Stable Boy:
David Mack

Stable Boy: David Mack

A Story of Struggle, Success, Shadow and Redemption

Joe Volk

ISBN: 978-0-578-81309-7

Library of Congress Cataloging-in-Publication Data

Name: Volk, Joe, 1961 - author
Title: Stable Boy: David Mack — A Story of Struggle, Success,
Shadows, and Redemption/ Joe Volk
Description: First edition.

Cover Design: Madelyn Bryan

Table of Contents

Thank you

From Joe:

First and foremost, to David for entrusting me with his story. It has been an honor and a privilege to tell it.

To all of the people in David's life that I've been fortunate to talk with and who have shared so many of their stories about David.

To Greg Hitchcock and Joe Douglas for the missing results culled from decades old newspaper clippings and SMTC computer files.

To Trish Porter Topmiller for the help with editing and encouragement.

To Don Strametz, Tony Yeoman, Russel Wong, and Don Chadez for the photos from David's running career.

To Jim Meyer, Michael Wing, and all my colleagues and students at St. Mary's who have encouraged and supported me with this project.

To my wife, Susan, and kids who listened to my nightly reading of these stories and encouraged me to keep going.

To my daughter, Madeline, who has always been by my side listening to my stories.

To my daughter and literary executrix, Emily, who inspired me to take on this project and who taught me the value of storytelling.

To my Dad, George, who was my first writing teacher, and who exposed me to Great Books as a kid.

From David:

First of all, no one makes it alone. That's a big misnomer in this country. It's a sad image that our country portrays — pull yourself up by the bootstraps. It's not true. No one pulls themselves up by the bootstraps. I didn't do it alone. There are so many people who helped me along the way. Whether it was words of encouragement, like Stram used to always say, "David, if you don't improve your grades, I don't care how fast you run, you won't get a scholarship to Tijuana Tech." Coach Yeoman and Coach Strametz had such a positive and profound impact on my life. They were polar opposites of one another. Yeoman was my cross country coach and Strametz my track coach. Moreover, they were life coaches. I will never forget the sincere kindness extended to me by Yeoman. I was so poor, he would pick me up for school because I could not afford a bus pass. He eventually paid for my monthly bus pass. I grew up so poor, yet I was rich with kindness, generosity, and genuine concern for my well being.

It's just people along the way, like Bill Dellinger pulling me aside and saying, "You're going to be successful," and I'm thinking he's talking about in track because I worked hard and trained hard, but he tells me, "No, you're going to be successful in life, and I just wanted you to know that." I never forgot those words.

There have always been people that cared. People like Joe Douglas, who was like a father to me and never wavered in his friendship and support of me.

Or Mrs. Reece, and the people who have shown me compassion, guidance, and love along the way that kept me encouraged to never give up and to know that people cared.

Thank you for the humanity that was shown to me by so many people throughout my life. I want people to know that it's the little things that count in life.

I want to give thanks to people who have their own mind, and not be so influenced by the media, and who think for themselves.

i

Preface
How I came to write this

On Sunday nights during my year at the University of Oregon, the cafeteria didn't serve dinner. I was never sure if this was a cost saving method for the student services department or if it was some grand design to get students off campus at least once a week to explore other culinary options within walking distance of student housing. I would periodically treat myself to a piece of pizza at the legendary Track Town Pizza across the street from campus. Back in the fall of 1979, Track Town Pizza had been open for only two years, but it had established itself as the place for track crazed fans and pilgrims to grab a piece of pizza or sandwich and enjoy the ambiance.

One Sunday night in the late fall I ventured over to grab a slice and spend some time admiring the University of Oregon and Olympic track stars' pictures that adorned the walls. Little did I realize that this particular Sunday would be the night that I would meet a Duck track icon and form a bond of friendship that has lasted these almost 40 years. "Hey, aren't you David Mack? I saw you race when you were in high school at Locke," I introduced myself.

David Mack had not yet run a race for the University of Oregon, but I had followed his career as our time in high school had coincided. That is quite an exaggeration though as his and my high school running careers could not be compared. My best placing was a narrow second place finish just ahead of an up-and-coming Serra freshman in a 2 mile in a home dual meet. David, a two-time California state 880 yard champion, ran 1:50.2 in winning his 1979 state title. His high school coaches at Locke, Don Strametz and Tony Yeoman, had guided him along brilliantly and with great care. Unlike many half milers, David had amazing versatility. His senior year, he ran 15:44 on the hilly Pierce Community College XC course, and just a few months later won the Muhammad Ali Indoor High School 1500m beating some of the best high school runners at the time. David's 3:50.8 beat good friend Jeff West of Crenshaw High School (2nd), his soon-to-be Oregon teammate Jeff Nelson of Burbank High School (3rd), University High School mile star Paul Medvin (4th), and Chuck Assumma of Eisenhower High School (5th). On May 6th of his senior season, David competed alongside some of the biggest names of the men's 800 meters at the Pepsi Invitational at Drake Stadium. David found himself right in the mix with Olympians Mike Boit and James Robinson.

Although we had never met before, our common bond of high school running in Southern California, and our love of track helped us hit it off immediately. David was extremely friendly and talkative. He joked about the transition from training as a half miler in an LA City school versus coming to Oregon and putting in long runs of 10 miles under legendary Ducks coach Bill Dellinger.

As college freshmen who had wound their way up to the Pacific Northwest, we were definitely out of our element and looked forward to the upcoming Christmas Break, when we could get home to warmer and dryer weather. I offered to give David a ride back to Southern California for the eagerly anticipated break. He gratefully agreed and said he would try to find others to share the ride in order to split the cost of gas. After all, gas had soared to over a dollar a gallon, and the more people we could assemble, the less we would each have to pay. I had a 1968 Dodge window van that could hold many people. David lined up two other riders: Duck teammates Parrish Nixon and Jeff Norris. I found three: Guy Cooksey, who would travel down I-5 as far as Medford; Ray Trigg, a swimmer, who would get dropped off in Sacramento; and a third guy, a cyclist, I had found on the Ride Share board in the ERB Memorial Union building.

So after we had finished our classes on the Friday before the break, we gathered our caravan of seven travelers in the parking lot outside of Bean Complex. My van had two seats in the front and a bench in the back, so two people of our original group would have to sit on the floor. We bungeed the cyclist guy's bike to the roof. The radio didn't work too well, but we had an 8-track player. We made it to Medford around dinner time and dropped off Guy Cooksey, a former standout football player for the Medford High School Tornadoes. We made a quick gas and dinner stop, and I was surprised at the less than friendly reception from the servers at Wendy's. I didn't think much of it at the time, but our van load of six college students, a mix of both black and white young men, must have been quite a strange sight in this lumber town. Guy had told us that Southern Oregon was pretty conservative but didn't go into much detail. We found out later that Medford had been a Sundown City well into the late 60s. Being relatively oblivious to the sight we must have been, our having a snowball fight at a gas stop in Dunsmuir, CA nearly rallied the town's citizenry and would have surely landed us in trouble. We continued on through the night fueled by the sounds of Parliament and Sugar Hill Gang's recently released "Rapper's Delight". There was much laughter and storytelling, and the mood was light until we threw a rod and pulled over broken down at Twisselman Rd. just north of the Grapevine. A mere 160 miles from home, but we were stranded. We killed time with more stories; the cyclist guy got his bike down off the roof and took a ride. Fortunately, my dad and brother were home and could come pick us up. The van would be towed home by my neighbor who owned a garage and would do the necessary repairs.

David's return home caused him to rethink his decision to attend the University of Oregon. He had been recruited by many schools, but he decided on Oregon largely due to the guidance of his high school coach, Don Strametz, who felt he would shine in their program.

Oregon garnered one of the best recruiting classes that year: national 2-mile record holder, Jeff Nelson; Oakton, VA standout Jim Hill; Mack, and his cross-town rival nation leading half miler Jeff West. West eventually decided that he did not want to attend U of O and was released from his commitment and landed at UCLA. With his friend and rival leaving, David sought to be released, but head coach Dellinger refused to release him. He saw in David a rare blend of natural speed and the desire to enjoy doing the longer runs. He recognized that David could be something special in the middle distance running world. David recognized in Dellinger a coach that could bring him to great things, "The only reason I'm still here is the coach" Mack said in a 1980 *Eugene Register Guard* article describing the tenuous relationship between himself and the University of Oregon, "I really like the coaching I'm getting, and that's what I'm here for. But just the coaching."

David's freshman year of college proved to be quite successful. Even as a rookie, he enthusiastically led a Duck team who were without upperclassmen leaders Alberto Salazar and Rudy Chapa, who were foregoing the 1980 season to focus on the upcoming Moscow Olympics. David's sensational performances in the 800m, 4x400, and occasional 1500m made him a Duck crowd favorite. He won his first of three Pac-10 800m titles over UCLA's Jeff West, and in the heat and humidity of Austin, TX David finished 6th in his first collegiate national championship meet. He capped his first collegiate season campaign by placing 6th in the Olympic Trials 800m in front of his hometown Duck crowd.

Bill Dellinger's coaching had done well for David who recognized this and after much deliberation would return his sophomore year. "The coach has done so good by me, everything he's done has been good, I trust whatever he tells me," he told Register Guard reporter John Conrad. I, on the other hand, felt the draw of being back closer to home and family didn't return and ended up at LMU my sophomore year. While I had personal success in my own running at LMU, I still felt compelled to follow the Ducks and David's successes. Over the next two years, David won two more Pac-10 800 meter titles and in 1982 even won a national title his junior year in the rarefied air of Provo, Utah. Unfortunately, for Dellinger, the Ducks, and the Ducks fans, David did leave Eugene and returned back home to Southern California.

Upon returning to Southern California after his junior year in 1982, David re-connected with Joe Douglas of the Santa Monica Track Club, where he would join a tremendous group of America's best middle distance talent to train with. David's good fortune of being coached by great coaches continued under the tutelage of Douglas. Over the next several years David qualified for two World Championship teams (Helsinki '83 and Rome '87), garnered the #1 US ranking for the 800m ('83), and ran on the US record setting 4x800m relay team splitting a 1:46.7 at the Mt. SAC Relays in April of 1986. During the 1985 season he recorded the then 2nd fastest American time for 800m of 1:43.35 and spoke about running even faster. He felt he was capable of running 1:41, a time which only five men in the world have ever accomplished. Surrounded by an amazing coach and a tremendous group for support few could argue that his goal was not within the realm of possibility.

Unfortunately, for David, his running career was cut short by illness and injury, but he turned this misfortune into an opportunity to pursue another of his interests; law enforcement. Even during his first years at the University of Oregon, David had wanted to pursue classes in criminology. He envisioned a post-athletics career in the FBI or as a parole officer. He went through the academy and joined the LAPD in 1988 as a step to pursuing this dream.

After our time together at the University of Oregon, our friendship consisted mostly of seeing each other periodically at local meets, and me following his successes through articles in the *L.A. Times* and *Track and Field News*. By the time David had joined the LAPD, I had moved back to Oregon.

David's life took a turn for the worse during these years, and I read with disbelief of the things written about him in the *L.A. Times* articles and other media outlets. The things I read about him seemed like a completely different person from the person I had known decades earlier. I certainly don't mean to gloss over those years of his life, but there has been enough written about him that anyone with any interest can certainly seek them out and find them. His vilification in the media saddens me to this day.

As we have reconnected these past few years, I am moved by the person I see. In a recent conversation, he wrote to me: "I like the adage that a friend is someone who knows you and still likes you. Thus I appreciate your kind words. Especially in light of the demonization of my character by the media. Thank you for caring enough to look beyond the B.S. to see the man you once knew as a very young man."

David has inspired me to be a better person. Even though we all live through dark moments in our lives, I can never imagine the things he has experienced, but I can look at the current life he is seeking to live and find the goodness in that. In a recent conversation with David, I told him: "As a Catholic and as a human being I am a big believer in redemption and forgiveness. I believe that we are not going to be judged by our worst moment of our lives but by what we become out of those moments. I certainly don't think we are made better by what the media foists on us, and I am glad that we are not judged by them."

I look at what David is doing and it is impressive. He has received a degree in Electronics and taught classes in Photovoltaics. He is working in renewable energy. He has become a community organizer and worked at the grassroots level for Vermont Senator Bernie Sanders' election to president during the 2016 presidential primaries. With his belief in giving back to his community, David has begun speaking to at-risk young men in the hopes that his experience can offer them a different path for their lives.

After breaking his pelvis and dislocating his hip after a fall from a roof while doing solar panel installation work, he began riding a stationary bike for physical therapy. Out of his rehabilitation, he took up cycling and has begun racing competitively. He rides for Bahati Cycling Club, which strives to build community and support youth programs through cycling.

In November of 2011 David suffered one of his biggest heartbreaks when his 25 year old son was killed while riding his motorcycle by an intoxicated driver. Out of the tragedy, David embarked on helping to raise the children of his son as his own. David's grandchildren are his pride and joy.

As I look at the totality of David's life I can't help but think of the ancient story of Odysseus, the terribly flawed but well traveled Greek hero. I recall a passage from a short story by Philip K. Dick that reminds me of David's journey, "Odysseus wanders as an individual, aware of himself as such. This is the idea of separation, of separation from family and country. The process of individuation. But Odysseus returns to his home. ...Finally, he goes home. ...As must all creatures. The moment of separation is a temporary period, a brief journey of the soul. It begins, it ends. The wanderer returns to land and race...."

His life's story is an inspiration, and I am honored to be able to tell the story of a man who has lived many lives and touched many people in his five plus decades on this planet. In his own reflections, "I am so at that point where dying is not even a concern of mine. We all know that it's going to happen; I'm not worried about it. I have lived a full life, and in many people's opinions, I've lived three lives,"

Chapter 1
Mark, Maurice, & Mack

So many times people think they possess knowledge of all there is to know about something and base their opinions on these assumptions, but in reality they never know the whole story. For instance, many people's preconceived notions of Compton, California focuses on images of gangs, guns, crime, and the ghetto. Those same people might be surprised to learn that in addition to the countless famous sports, artistic and music stars like tennis champions Venus and Serena Williams; Olympic long jump gold medalist and world record holder Bob Beamon; Grammy award winning Blues musician Keb' Mo'; ABC *Black-ish* star Anthony Anderson; and rapper/songwriter Kendrick Lamar there are also numerous others like Academy Award winning actor/director Kevin Costner; NFL commissioner Pete Rozelle; former 41st President and First Lady George H.W. Bush and Barbara Bush; or legendary actress Marilyn Monroe who were born or lived in Compton. Likewise, for many but those who might have grown up in Compton, few know of its rural boundaries that lay at the outskirts of the city.

In 1867 Griffith Compton left the gold rush boom around Stockton and headed south settling south of downtown Los Angeles. The farming life for Compton and the thirty other settlers faced hardships, but they eventually decided to incorporate the land into the city of Compton. Griffith donated his land in exchange for an agreement that a portion of his land would be zoned agricultural. This farmland attracted the black families who had begun migrating from the rural South in the 1950s, and there they found their 'home away from home'. Compton couldn't support large-scale agricultural business, but it did give the residents the opportunity to work the land for their families.

For David Mack, growing up in Compton in the 1960s and 1970s, these Richland Farms horse properties provided an outlet for a life in the ghetto. At age ten, David and his friends Mark and Maurice decided that they wanted to ride horses. They hung out at a stable on East El Segundo Blvd. in Compton hoping for the chance to ride. They spent their time after school sitting on the fence near the corals asking the stable hands if they could help in exchange for riding the horses. Finally, one day one of the stable hands told the boys that they could ride if they would work in the stables shoveling the manure. A few hours into their work, Mark and Maurice realized that this was

1

too much for them and left David to shovel the stalls by himself. Unafraid of hard work, he wanted to ride, and this labor provided his chance to prove to the stable hand that he could handle the task.

After his apprenticeship as a stable boy, he had earned the chance to ride. He loved the sensation of freedom on the horses Snowflake and Smokey. With that freedom also came injury. One day while working in the corrals, David jumped off a corral gate landing on a 2x4 with a rusty nail and punctured his foot. The follow-up visit to the doctor brought more bad news. The doctor told him that the injury to his foot would make him always walk with a limp. From early on in David's life, he would not let misfortune consume him. Instead he would take misfortune, turn it around, and make it into something better.

Chapter 2
The Childhood Years

Our stories shape who we are. Like a tapestry, sometimes by just looking at the backside we can't see the beauty of the complicated design in life. By flipping it around we can enjoy the beauty present before our eyes. Our life's stories are intricately woven together to make this life that we have. Each person in our lives, each event, and even every seemingly random moment become the threads of this spectacular tapestry. We shouldn't focus on the backside and see the jumbled mess that these crisscrossed individual threads display. Instead, we must try to see the amazing artwork that our stories hold.

David's life story begins in a somewhat crisscrossed and jumbled way. He recalls that his first childhood memory was seeing his mom, a short Hispanic woman with long dark hair, cooking for him and his five siblings, who all slept on two bunk beds in the family's small house near 116th and Mona in Compton. David, whose birth name was Angel, later learned that his mom had become pregnant with three of the children by an African American man, whereas the other three siblings had a father who was Mexican. In 1963, David's mom decided to return to Mexico, but since racism was prevalent in Mexico, she decided to only take the three children who were full Mexican. David and his other two mixed siblings were given to neighbors. David ended up with Harrison and Joyce Mack; neighbors across the street. Still to this day, David is not sure where his brother and sister ended up. It is from Harrison that David would be given the name David Lorenzo Mack.

While one can never truly understand what deep seated impact being given up by his mother had on him, it proved to be another thread in the tapestry of his life. David harbors no ill-feeling toward his biological mom. "She could have very easily aborted me or left me in a garbage can. Instead, I was given life, and it was up to me to make use of what I'd been given. In life you have to find reasons to succeed and not fail. We've all had dysfunctional or traumatic experiences in our lives, and you can concentrate on that or fixate on that, or you can move on in life and enjoy that you're here."

David recalls that when he first joined the Mack household, it was like a birthday party celebration for him. Having grown up speaking Spanish in his

3

mom's house, he knew no English, and called his new mother "Joyce" because that is what everyone else was calling her. He remembers that she did not like this and beat him demanding to be called "mom".

David speaks of Joyce being illiterate, a go-go dancer, and part-time prostitute; her story would shape the fabric of David's. In the days before tax funded free lunches for school kids, David had to take his wagon and find food in trash cans and dumpsters because Joyce provided little help for David's nutritional or educational needs. David recalls thinking, "I can remember walking down the street being hungry, and I would look at adults and wonder why they wouldn't give me some food or care. They didn't know, but as a kid, you don't know that they don't know. You just think you're a pitiful sight, 'Don't you know? Can't you see that I'm hungry? Can't you see that I'm cold.'"

Fifty-eight years of life experience gives David the opportunity to reflect on his own poverty and offer some insights for today, "We all have to come together as people and realize that we are all human beings, and that's all that matters. Everybody's suffering, and whether you know it or not, you are suffering with those kids in detention centers, with people who are homeless, or with those people living under the freeway. We are all suffering, and, obviously, they are suffering more from the physical and emotional neglect, but we are suffering from seeing it and feeling inadequate because we don't know what to do to help. It's human nature to want to help; your natural instinct is to go help. Unfortunately, we have become hamstrung in not knowing how to help, and we are constantly being bombarded with the message that 'these people' are not worthy of being helped. They're immigrants or they're brown people, who are to be looked down upon. Or these homeless people are drug addicts, so they're sub-human. No! These are human beings, and we want to help. We are all suffering, whether we know it or not."

David recollects that Joyce would tell him that if he needed or wanted something, he could steal it instead of her giving him money from the welfare that she collected for her dependents. This neglect would not beat him but make him stronger, "I learned at an early age how to survive. And this was a part of my life that formed and shaped me. She had shown me that if that is what you want, then that's how you go and get it. I can remember that when I was growing up and being poor that if I wanted new shoes or something Joyce would tell me, 'Stop the fucking crying, and you go in there and steal them.' It didn't justify anything later on in life, but my whole value system was kind of fucked up to begin with."

One thing that David is grateful for from Joyce is the gift of his Grandmother Margaret Smiley. "She had a profound effect on me by showing me affection and love, which I didn't have."

Theologian Thomas Aquinas, in his *Summa Theologia*, expresses the belief that humans are "both saints and sinners". This dichotomy would permeate David's lifetime experiences. Oftentimes in life we lean towards one of these inclinations depending on the circumstances of life or perhaps the company we keep and the influence they have on us. Growing up in Compton would shape David's life. In addition to the feeling of freedom that he would gain from riding horses at the stables off East El Segundo Blvd., he would also experience the impact of the racial tension and police brutality as witnessed in the Watts Riots of August of 1965 just three miles away. Following those riots CIA Director, John McCone, would issue a report at the request of Governor Pat Brown. According to *L.A. Times* reporter, Darrell Dawsey, "The McCone Commission identified the root causes of the riots to be high unemployment, poor schools, and related inferior living conditions that were endured by African Americans in Watts. Recommendations for addressing these problems included 'emergency literacy and preschool programs, improved police-community ties, increased low-income housing, more job-training projects, upgraded health-care services, more efficient public transportation, and many more.' Most of these recommendations were never implemented."

In the late 60s and early 70s, David remembers benefitting from the Black Panthers' Free Breakfast for School Children Program over on Stockwell St.. According to Erin Blakemore: "Free Breakfast For School Children was one of the most effective [social programs of the Black Panthers]. It began in January 1969 at an Episcopal church in Oakland, and within weeks it went from feeding a handful of kids to hundreds. The program was simple: party members and volunteers went to local grocery stores to solicit donations, consulted with nutritionists on healthful breakfast options for children, and prepared and served the food free of charge." David recalls that they played motivational speeches on reel to reel tape players, and even though they were "way too advanced for our little brains, they were feeding our souls and our bodies. What I didn't understand at the time, but our subconscious mind absorbed that, so I was revolutionized at an early age."

David's childhood became fraught with peril and instability. In the first of many incidents throughout his life where David faced his own mortality, he was but a young child. With essentially no parental guidance, he took on the responsibility of caring for himself. Joyce would often leave him to fend for himself while she went out and partied. One particular rainy night, when David was eight years old, he remembers that Joyce had gone out and his pet cat began to meow to get let in from the rain. David obliged, dried it off with a towel, and let it sleep on the bed with him, but upon Joyce's returning after 2:30 in the morning, she saw that David's cat was inside. "She kicked me and the cat out at 3:00 in the morning. So I walked about three miles in the rain to my Godmother's [Marie Madarang], house. She lived in an apartment upstairs, so I banged on the door, but she couldn't hear me because of the rain. I was cold and wanted to get inside, so I got up on the carport and began to climb in through their kitchen window. My Godfather was like, 'Hold it right there, or I'll shoot you!' My Godmother came in and yelled at my Godfather, 'Put that goddamn gun down! That's David.' My own Godfather almost shot me. He thought I was a burglar breaking in. Welcome to my life."

David's grandmother, Margaret Smiley, pictured here with his Aunt Maude, provided him with a loving maternal presence that he lacked growing up.

Chapter 3
The School Years

Because of the transitory nature of his home life, David lived in several houses growing up in Compton: 116th and Mona; East Bliss Street (he actually lived in three houses on this block); Aranbe Avenue; East Spruce Street; and East Oris Street. And he attended numerous elementary schools: Marian Anderson Elementary; George Washington Elementary; Dickerson Elementary; and John F. Kennedy Elementary. The constant moving impacted David's education and created a sense of instability in his life.

Sometimes our stories overlap with each other; one thread of our life's tapestry tugging on another one. One such story that David recalls from his early days in school occurred during his second or third grade. Although it rarely rains in Southern California, when it does rain it comes down in torrents. Because of the neglect of Joyce, David went to school one rainy day in nothing but a t-shirt, shorts, and ragged shoes. He arrived sopping wet and shivering at Mrs. Reece's classroom, and she jumped up, hugged him in tears. Upset that he would be sent to school without a jacket to protect against the rain, she took him to the office to get him dry clothes. David says, "She called Children's Welfare Services; she called everybody but the president."

Social workers came and they took him to get clothes. When Children's Welfare visited Joyce, she was told that if David showed up to school without weather appropriate clothes again, she would be arrested. David remembers the trouble this caused, "I became a double victim— with this alcoholic beating me for getting her in trouble." In order to protect David from Joyce's abuse, Mrs. Reece took it upon herself to bring clothes that her son had grown out of for David.

As sometimes happens in our stories, those threads on the back of the tapestry become tangled, and we are never aware of how some little moment might have an impact later in our lives. David was able to see the completion of the circle of the impact that Mrs. Reece had on his life when he was working undercover for the LAPD twenty years later. "We are doing a sting operation where we first come in and scoop up the local drug dealer. Then we pose as the drug dealer and scoop up the buyers. One of the guys that comes up to buy from me turns out to be Mrs. Reece's son. When they wrapped him all up, I'm looking at him in handcuffs, and I asked him, 'What's your name? Is your mom a teacher?'

The man replied, 'Yes, she's retired. You know Mrs. Reece?'

"I say, 'Goddammit! This is your lucky day. You have no idea how sweet your mom was to me, and I'm sure it breaks your momma's heart to know that you're out here buying drugs. Your mom used to give me your old clothes, and that's how sweet she was.' I said, 'Turn him loose; I must've made a mistake on this one.'"

"So I paid it forward, and he told me that she still lived at the same address, so I went to visit her and told her. She thanked me, hugged me, and cried telling me how she wished she could get him off of drugs."

Despite the difficult and transitory childhood life that David had been thrust into, he refused to be beaten by his circumstances but instead this resulted in him finding a friend, Ronald Gaines, who would serve as classmate, teacher, mentor, and surrogate brother to him. Having grown up in a Spanish speaking household for his developmental years, and then not having family support to teach him to read, he was essentially illiterate until eighth grade. "He helped me to learn how to read in the summer transition from the seventh to the eighth grade. We were polar opposites. He was an honor roll student. He believed in God. But most of all he was my friend. And that is all that really matters," says David.

One of the stories that David remembers reading from this period in his life, "Flowers For Algernon" by Daniel Keyes, resonated with him because the protagonist, Charlie Gordon, couldn't read but eventually gains phenomenal intelligence through a surgical technique. With Ronald's help, David would begin to turn around the deficits that had beset his early childhood. As he began to read more and more, he read anything he could get his hands on. The impact that Ronald had on fostering a love for reading in David would continue on well into later years of his life.

In addition to being his friend/teacher/mentor, David also worked with Ronald's uncle doing odd jobs around the neighborhood. David recounts a story told to him by Ronald's mother, Katherine, who David still keeps in touch with. "One morning I was waiting outside my house down on East 130th Street and South Aranbe Avenue getting ready to go to work waiting for Ronald's uncle to come pick me up for some construction work when a car came down the street and came to a stop at the stop sign. Then tires began spinning, and it is now going in reverse into the school's [Anderson Elementary] parking lot basically going in circles in reverse. In what seemed like slow motion, I saw the door of the woman's car come open like she was trying to get out to escape. By now she has backed out back into the street. It was traveling in reverse towards a "No Parking" sign, and her leg got trapped between her car door and the sign severing the woman's lower leg from the rest of her body. I'm watching all this as it is happening, as if it was in slow motion. After being dragged in the street she hops up to the grass at Ronald's house on one leg. I instinctively start walking toward her slowly, thinking, 'What the hell's going on?' but she's screaming, 'My baby! My baby!' Except the car is still going in reverse doing circles. She's screaming because her baby, who had been trapped in the car, has now been thrown from the car into the street. The baby is standing up in the street, and I rushed back over towards the car not even thinking about my own safety. I grabbed her baby from the path of the car just as it was about to run it over. As I stood up, I felt the bumper of the car touch my butt. It eventually crashed into a telephone pole and the engine was still roaring with the tires in motion. Not only had I saved the baby's life, but I had risked my own life in doing so. I brought it to her, and seeing that the baby was okay helped to calm her down a bit. Ronald's step-dad, Orry Winfield, ran out responding to the sound of squealing and screaming. He starts helping the woman and begins instructing me to hold her leg, but I'm just a fourteen year old boy, and I'm doing my best just trying not to throw up at the sight of her severed leg. You've got the bone sticking out. You've got veins and all this blood. My hands are getting submerged in blood, and he's trying to get the tourniquet tied on to save her life because her femoral artery had been cut. The sheriffs came before the ambulance came, and they just put her, her leg, and the baby in the car and took off."

This story of the fine balance between life and death had long been forgotten by David until Katherine reminded him some forty-three years later. David takes the opportunity to use that story to express concern about the world he grew up in, "If that story had happened anywhere else, there would be news teams down there. The fire chief, the police chief, and the mayor would be down there recognizing the heroics of Mr. Winfield and me. Urban blight! People just didn't care about what was going on in the ghetto."

David's encountering that fine balance of life and death became commonplace. One day while waiting outside a laundromat, one of Mr. Winfield's sons pulled out a shotgun and killed another man coming out of the laundromat. David remembers that he felt compelled to have to tell Orry Winfield of what he had just witnessed, and that his son had just killed someone.

Sometimes that fine balance involved David's life being in the crosshairs. Another incident where David almost lost his life happened when he was twelve years old. Riding his bike around his neighborhood on El Segundo Blvd., he paused to wait for a driver at an intersection. The driver motioned him to cross and David began. The driver hit the gas and drove right over David and his bike. He careened out of control driving into a house across the street. Eyewitnesses ran to the car to pull David out from under the car fearing that he surely had been killed having been dragged the twenty-five yards into the side of the house. The man, who was obviously drunk, was pulled out of his car by several of the neighbors, while others were searching under the chassis trying to rescue David. By some miracle, the car had driven over David and his bike, but had not dragged him across the intersection, the sidewalk, and the person's yard. David, who was banged up, but relatively unphased was more concerned about who was going to replace his damaged bicycle. "That guy never did get me a new bike," David recalls forty-five years later.

One of the saving graces of David's junior high years at Willowbrook Junior High was his introduction to organized running. His P.E. teacher encouraged him to join the track team. David agreed to give it a try, and when asked what event he wanted to do, David emphatically replied that he wanted to be a distance runner. This meant that David would run the 1320 yard run. His success over three laps was immediate as he won each race that he ran. That was until his final race of his junior high career.

In addition to running, David participated in martial arts as a youth. On the morning of his final meet, he got into a fight with a fellow student, and in the process of the fight had kicked the boy in the butt. Even though he had vanquished the boy, the kick had caused the instep of his foot to swell. He ran nonetheless, but finished dead last hobbled by the injured foot. He sat on the infield and cried tears of pain and sadness. His coach consoled him reminding him that this was only one race and that, prophetically, there would be many others in the years to come.

David would also join a youth track club out of Long Beach along with soon-to-be sprint sensations James Sanford (1977 California State 400 meter and 4x400 relay state champion for Pasadena High School) and his brother Michael (1978 & 1979 California State 200 meter champion). David's early success would catch the eye of Westchester High School and Santa Monica Track Club coach, Joe Douglas, "I remember watching him, and I thought he had very good mechanics and very good speed. I remember telling him that I thought he could be a very good runner."

Growing up in Compton with the danger of gang violence in his neighborhood and the neglect that Joyce brought to David's world eventually caused him to run away to live with his Godmother. Joyce had a co-worker that had fled her pimp, and she landed at David's house. She sexually molested David when he was in the eighth grade, and David realized that Joyce would offer no protection or support.

The final straw came when he and Ronald were nearly killed by gang members. During junior high school, David had been hanging out with a friend in the neighborhood, Lloyd, who was a little older than David. Lloyd was a member of a gang, and David saw himself as a wannabe gang member— a hanger on. "One time this guy came and said, 'Hey, the police got Lloyd, and his mom wants you to come up there and tell them that he was with you so they won't take him to jail.'

"I said, 'Okay,' but I was at Ron's house, so I had him ride me to Lloyd's house on the handlebars of his bike. It was around 9:30 at night, but as we were getting closer to Lloyd's house I could see the silhouette of some of these guys, and I knew that these guys were enemies of mine and Lloyd. So I told Ron, 'Turn around! Turn around! It's a set-up. As soon as he turned the bike around they blasted at us with a shotgun. BOOM! BOOM! We were so far away that the pellets just grazed us in the back. I went home that night and packed my little duffle bag and I was gone. Ran away. Gone. I left Compton and went to stay with my Godmother in Los Angeles.

David knew that his only way to survive was to run. His move to his Godmother's would mean that he would attend Locke High School instead of Centennial High School, where he would have surely remained a target of those guys who wanted to kill him. Out of all the bad happening in David's world, this move would remind him of the life lesson, "In life you have to find reasons to succeed and not to fail."

Chapter 4
The High School Years

David's rise from illiteracy, poverty, and the climb out of the ghetto began slowly during his high school years. Attending Locke High School, David, although still struggling academically, would soon learn valuable lessons outside of the classroom. His high school coach, Don Strametz remembers that getting David to come out for track was not an immediate decision on David's part, "I remember watching him run around the track during sixth period gym class with Tony Yeoman, who was coaching with me at that time, and we just shook our heads. This kid had so much natural talent out there. He was just breezin' along with this really good stride, and he had this little ponytail bouncing along. We walked up to him and said that we thought it would be great if he would become a part of the track team. He said that he was a drummer in a band and that he didn't have time for track. We kept after him, and after about three weeks, we convinced him to give it a try."

Coach Strametz and Coach Yeoman found an invitational for him, the Burbank Relays, and once David started running, he liked it. Then it was just a matter of trying to keep him healthy. He had been living in a shack in the back of his Godmother's place where the only heating was the stove that he cooked his food on. Coach Strametz recalls, "He wasn't as well nourished as he should have been especially for someone who had started to train for track. We were able to get him signed up for the free breakfasts that the school provided to be sure that he was getting a square meal in him because we weren't sure how many other square meals he was getting at the time. I think it was a member of the cafeteria staff called me and said, 'You better check on David because he had what looked to be bite marks on his face from what looked like had been a rat.'"

Since David had only recently become a reader thanks to the help of Ronald Gaines during junior high, David became a voracious reader in the tenth grade. With his newfound introduction to running, it was only natural that he would blend these two loves, "As a late-bloomer in learning how to read late, I just started reading everything like Charlie [from "Flowers From Algernon"]. I just couldn't get enough of it as the world opened up to me. I found a book on the life of Jim Ryun [Cordner Nelson's *The Jim Ryun Story*]. I read what he was doing [for training], and I started trying to emulate that."

David remembers that in the first chapter of the book, Ryun was referred to as "The Ugly Duckling," and David saw parallels in the two of them being marginalized for the circumstances of their very different lives. Inspired by the hard work of the mile world record holder, David decided to be like Ryun, and he "started hammering." One of the training runs that David did was to run the length of El Segundo Blvd. from Compton to the beach in El Segundo and back, 23.4 miles roundtrip. This was in the days before Casio watches, so he had no idea how far it was or what training methodology he was following, but it did help forge his mental toughness that would be a hallmark of his running career.

One of the things that became a positive characteristic in David's life was the introduction of good people into his life just when he needed it most. He found this from his Grandmother Margaret "Grammy" Smiley, Godmother Marie Madarang, Katherine and Ronald Gaines when he was a school aged child, and now he was finding it as a high school athlete from his coaches and teammates. Like his birth name, Angel, David would find the presence of these good people to help provide him with comfort, protection, patience, redemption, unconditional love, and purpose. Coach Tony Yeoman purchased David a city bus pass since David was out of the district attending Locke High School. Tony recalls, "He didn't have much of a home life, so when he was moving from place to place with whichever relative was providing him with a place to stay, I would come by and pick him up quite often. I developed quite a relationship with him driving in and discussing quite a few things like making sure he was keeping up with his school work. He was just a really neat kid."

Strametz agrees that the presence of teammates and coaches brought out the best in David, "I never heard him once swear. I never heard him once belittle anybody. I never heard him put down anybody. He was always encouraging especially to the younger athletes. He was just a good solid kid, who had a real rough upbringing."

As a member of the Locke High School Saints track team, David learned and then proceeded to share the value of diligence, hard work and dealing with setbacks. As a sophomore, David excelled right off and won the L.A. City "B" title for the 880 yards.

During his sophomore year, David had, yet again, another brush with death. While attending a house party, a group of jocks from a neighboring school believed that the girl, a cheerleader at their school, that David had come to the party with should not be giving her attention to him. One of the jocks pulled a gun on David and threatened to kill him. David's quick thinking girlfriend, protected his life by telling them that he was her cousin.

At the 1978 Arcadia Invitational during his junior year his win over Jeff West and Johnny Gray would set the tone for their many years rivalry. Their races were the stuff of legend, as the meet program of the Arcadia Invitational recalls, "David Mack, who would run sub-1:50 in a great race the next year [1979] with Jeff West, took the Boys 800 at 1:53.6"

David's teammate, Leonard Miller, also a half miler and member of the mile relay team, who was a senior during David's junior year saw him as "intense, even as a kid. He would go to school early in the morning to get in an extra workout before school even started. And then he would do the regular practice after school with the team. That's how David became so good. He was driven. David wanted to win at all costs. He went above and beyond in everything he did." Even though Leonard would graduate a year ahead of David, they would remain friends over the next forty years and eventually became co-workers with the LAPD ten years after high school.

David concluded his junior year by winning the California State 880 yards title. According to Keith R. Conning of *Highlights of the California State Track Meet*, "The 880 produced one of the most exciting races of the meet as underclassmen ended 1-2-3. David Mack of Locke, L.A. won in 1:51.83 over soph Pete Quinonez of Tulare Union (1:51.91) and junior Jeff West of Crenshaw, L.A. (1:52.04). One of the favorites, Mike White of Richmond, finished fourth in 1:52.51."

In addition to racing well and winning titles, David had become a leader. His Locke teammate and good friend, Gary Kelly, says of David, "I learned a hell of a whole lot from David as an athlete. His intensity, his drive and work ethic was, bar none, the most impressive I've ever encountered in my life. He would not accept any excuses. It did not matter what the weather was like. If Coach Stram called off practice because of bad weather, David would get us together and get in a cross country run or interval work in the hallways. And if he had to work out by himself, he would. It would inspire us to be the best that we could be."

David's impact on Gary would be long lasting. Because of the example for his Saints teammates, Gary upon enrolling at UC Berkeley, and because of David's encouragement, ended up walking on for the Cal Bears track team. Gary credits David's inspiration for him to be able to lower his quarter mile time from 49.2 at Locke to 46.50 as a freshman at Cal. The former high school teammates would bring out the best in each other as Pac-10 competitors during their college careers. Gary recalls the Pac-10 championship meet their junior year of college, "At the University of Oregon that year, David and I were matched up in the mile relay. I got the stick ahead of him, but I knew he was coming, and he just blew by me. After being injured following my freshman year, it was David who encouraged me to keep it up."

Fellow Locke teammate, Archie Carter, has an additional perspective on David's impact on his teammates. Archie, who played football for Locke and eventually for Pasadena City College and University of Illinois, specialized in the open 100 and 220 yard dashes, and also ran on the Saints' nation leading mile relay team (3:13.1) speaks to how David brought out the best in him and his teammates, "Mack was a person who was always cool—never nervous; at least no one saw it in him. We didn't realize the legacy that we were starting, but we used to tell him, 'We're going to bring it to you. We aren't going to let anyone touch you; we're going to bring it to you. All you've got to do is bring it in. It wasn't boasting; we just hadn't yet realized that no one could beat us. It wasn't just how fast we were. We would see Valerie Brisco [Hooks] everyday at practice, who always won. That was the team mentality. 'We can't lose.' Every meet was, 'You got this? Yeah, let's bring this home.' We saw that in Mack. Mack never lost; so we never lost. If David had to give a lung up to win the 880, he gave a lung up. We all knew that he would fall on the track at the end of his 880, but he was still going to run the mile and anchor the mile relay. That's the reason why we all stuck together, because we knew Mack was tired, and we had to not bring it short. I would tell him, 'You'll never get this baton in second or third place.' We had that discipline to leave it all out there, and that was the discipline that made him a stronger man now."

In Latin, the word "competitor" means to bring out the best. David did just that with not just his teammates but two of his other friends and rivals, Crenshaw High School standouts, Jeff West and Johnny Gray. Since both

17

David and Jeff were in the same grade (class of '79), the same events (880 and 4x440), and the same CIF section (L.A. City) they faced each other numerous times a season (Locke vs. Crenshaw dual meets, invitationals, league championship meets, L.A. City Championships, and California State Championships). Their rivalry brought out the best in each other and would form a bond that would last well into their later lives.

Being a year older than David, Johnny Gray, found himself in an unusual position of looking up to the younger runners. Gray had moved from Portland, Oregon the middle of his junior year to Crenshaw High School, where he competed in football and basketball. Urged by the Crenshaw High School track coach, Merle McGee, Johnny joined the track team to get in shape for football and basketball. Gray focused on the two mile but didn't really enjoy running. He saw, in Mack and West though, an escape from having to race eight laps. "They ran the half mile, and that was only two laps. I decided I wanted to run the half mile. I ran 2:17 [debut season as a junior], and Jeff was one of the best. So we would meet up with David over at Locke on the weekend and train together. David was a beast, and because these guys were younger than me, I said to myself, 'I can't let these younger guys beat me. I tried a little harder, but these guys were good. It wasn't easy for me, but I had the motivation from them. We were all friends, and they pushed me to run better and take it more seriously. When I broke 2:10, I was really happy, and then when I broke 2:00, I thought I was really good. They loved the sport so much, it made me take it more seriously. I didn't go out for football and basketball [his senior year]. We battled my senior year [1978], and I finally beat them at the L.A. City Championships running 1:54 something. I finished my senior year having run 1:51 and they had both run under 1:50. Everytime that they would run better would motivate me to run better.'"

After Johnny graduated in 1978, the bond between David and Jeff now even stronger, presented itself at the 1979 Muhammad Ali Indoor Invitational at the Long Beach Arena. Mack and West, two of the country's best high school half milers, found themselves entered in the 1500 meters against some of the country's best high school long distance runners. Being outside the high school season, CIF rules forbade the wearing of school uniforms during indoor invitationals. David and Jeff showed their bond of friendship by wearing the same singlet and shorts, and ended up finishing first (3:50.8) and second (3:50.9) against Jeff Nelson (3rd in 3:52.3), Paul Medvin (4th in 3:53.7), and Chuck Assumma (5th in 3:54.4). Nelson, who would break both Craig Virgin's outdoor and Gerry Lindgren's indoor national high school 2 mile records with his time of 8:36.3, would end up being a part of the University of Oregon's all-star recruiting class of '79/80 with David.

David's ability to succeed in the 880 and the longer races garnered the attention of several collegiate coaches. David even demonstrated his running prowess by racing an impressive 15:44 on the L.A. City Section Pierce Community College cross country course. At the 1979 Arcadia Invitational, the meet program recounts, "L.A. City rivals David Mack (Locke) and Jeff West (Crenshaw) met in a breath-taking 800, with Mack taking the win on the lean with both at 1:49.9 (MR). Their battle down the homestretch was a classic, and David later anchored a 3:13.1 MR 4x400 team. "

David's success during his senior year was not without difficulties. Even though he had run away to get away from the environment he was being brought up in before attending high school, his success had garnered the attention of Joyce. "During my senior year, I split time living with Joyce's boyfriend or my grandmother. I had to become an emancipated minor because Joyce had tried to prevent me from competing in the state championship track meet my senior year. She was a ghetto urchin and she didn't want to see me succeed. I had run away after ninth grade, and she heard about the success I was having. She was a vindictive snake. And that is what it is."

David saw in his grandmother someone who not only gave him love and affection, but also became the buffer between him and the many college coaches who wanted him to attend their colleges. David recalls, "She got the full brunt of these coaches calling trying to recruit me. They would talk to her and come by to visit. I got letters from everywhere: Georgetown, Tennessee, Villanova, UCLA, USC, Oregon… and I was just a kid and didn't know anything about track and its history. I'd be on the phone with Dellinger, and I wouldn't have anything to say, but she was just so proud that all these people wanted me-- this little ragamuffin. The irony was that she never saw me run. It just never occurred to me to ask her, but she wasn't mobile, having only one leg and all. She was so proud of me."

Growing up poor, David saw that his success in running might lead to bigger things. Archie Carter is quick to point out, "David would tell us, 'I'm the poorest,' but I was like, 'Oh, Mack, we all were poor.' We didn't tease each other about hair or clothing, or shoes, but whatever personal things he

19

had going on at home, he didn't bring to the track. We were like a family to each other. Living in Watts, it was very hard to get out, and track was our way of getting out. Being on track made us realize that we weren't 'poor'; we saw that there were no obstacles in front of us."

Despite the struggles, he finished his senior season by winning the L.A. City 880 yards title and another California State 880 yards title. According to Keith R. Conning of *Highlights of the California State Track Meet*, "The 880 was loaded! In addition to defending champion Mack, the 2nd and 3rd place finishers in 1978, Pete Quinonez (Tulare Union) and Jeff West (Crenshaw, L.A.), were also entered. The 880 turned out to be a two man race with David Mack of Locke, the defending champ, winning in 1:50.2 over Jeff West of Crenshaw (1:50.5). Third place went to Jim Brennan of El Camino, Oceanside in 1:52.3. Last year's runner-up, Pete Quinonez of Tulare Union, finished fourth in 1:53.0. Mack is only the fourth performer in meet history to win consecutive 880 titles. The last was Don Bowden of Lincoln, S.J. in 1953-54."

Bowden would go on to become the first American to break the sub-4 minute mile (3:58.7 in Stockton, CA in 1957). David Mack had become a member of an elite group of America's top high school half milers along with Jeff West, who led the nation with a 1:48.2 run during the summer after their senior year. Many collegiate coaches were quite interested in them.

Davi
d and Jeff's rivalry and friendship would make each other
two of the best runner in the US.

**David and Jeff would step up in distance to the 1500 meters
to face some of the best HS runners in the country.
Paul Medvin, Jeff Nelson, West and Mack lead the pack.**

Mack and West would go 1-2 against some of the best HS runners of the country at the 1979 Ali Indoor 1500 meters

David "bringing it home" as anchor for the Locke Saints

1979 Locke HS Mile Relay: Bobby Deary, Gary Kelly, Archie Carter, & David Mack would run a nation leading 3:13.1

Coach Tony Yeoman, David, and Coach Don Strametz at the 1979 track awards banquet

Jeff and David on the podium at the 1979 state meet.

Chapter 5
A Big Decision To Make:
880 miles From Compton to Eugene

David's successful high school career meant that many schools had taken an interest in him. He possessed tremendous speed as evidenced by his success in the 4x440 and 880 yards, but he also demonstrated success in the longer events as seen by his 3:50.8 time and victory in the Ali 1500 meters and his impressive 15:44 at Pierce Community College in the L.A. City XC Championships. Before his state 880 victory in 1979, Pepsi Invitational meet Director, Al Franken, invited David to compete alongside Olympians Mike Boit of Kenya and James Robinson of the USA on May 6th. As did several other California high school standouts such as Paul Medvin of University High School in the mile and Jeff Nelson of Burbank High School in the two mile, David's performance (1:51.6 for 9th place) in this invitational showed that he was more than ready for the next stage.

Mack and Nelson would make their recruiting trip to Eugene together, and this would make an impression not only on David but also on the future teammates and fans of Hayward Field. Springtime in Eugene is often quite rainy, and David, coming from Southern California, was not prepared for the wet weather. While on his weekend visit, he attended a Duck meet at Hayward Field. At this time David often wore his hair in a long braid. Greg Erwin recalls that David made quite an impression when he arrived, "He didn't have any rain gear, so someone gave him one of those yellow adidas rain jackets to borrow. He was running around in a t-shirt and shorts and that rain jacket with that long braid. I thought to myself, 'Holy smokes. Who is this guy?' He definitely looked different, and boy did he attract the attention of the people in Eugene. At that time, he was a foreign object in Eugene. But I distinctly remember that he was a fish out of water from South Central to Eugene, Oregon. He was a different cat coming to Eugene at that time."

According to Coach Strametz, "When David returned from his visit to Eugene, he was awestruck. He told me, 'Coach, they have a river running through their campus!'" Having grown up in South Central rivers and forests were quite foreign to David.

David saw himself attending USC, and his friend and rival, Jeff West, leaned toward UCLA. By staying in Southern California, David could remain close to his high school girlfriend, Florence Griffith, who had transferred to UCLA. University of Oregon coach, Bill Dellinger, indicated that he was interested in both David and Jeff. After much deliberation, they decided to attend the same school. "We came [to Oregon] as a package deal. They were able to give us both scholarships."

Coach Dellinger acknowledges that he knew of David's upbringing in poverty, troubled home life and eventual emancipation from Joyce Mack, but he saw in David a runner that could be amazing. He thought so highly of David and recognized in Mack the possibility of him becoming the next Prefontaine, "He was very good, and he was going to be even more than that."

David left for Eugene shortly after graduating from Locke High School. He found a job working at Consolidated Lumber out near the Eugene Airport to earn some money. He had been offered a room by future Duck teammate, Art Boileau, at the Sigma Chi House. Numerous Duck track stars such as Dyrol Burleson (former American mile and 1500 meters record holder), Roscoe Divine (former world 4x 1 mile record holder), Jerry Tarr (former 4x110 world record holder), and Les Steers (former high jump world record holder) had been Sigma Chi members. Dellinger, a former Sigma Chi fraternity member himself, knew of its availability during the summer months, which provided David with a place to live for the summer until he could get into the dorms. His summer of working and running prepared him for the collegiate life. As other athletes began showing up, he heard that his friend Jeff West had gotten cold feet.

Over the summer Jeff began to have second thoughts, so he sought to get released from his commitment. When Dellinger agreed to release Jeff, David notified Bill that he, too, would like to be released and was ready to take a bus home after the initial weeks of fall practice. "The University [of Oregon] wouldn't let me out of mine, so I felt captive. I always wanted to go to SC but Coach Strametz wanted me to go here. So I did that because he asked me to."

One of David's Duck teammates let Dellinger know that he was planning to go home, and Bill met David at the Eugene Greyhound station. David recalls the conversation, "I was getting ready to get on the bus [to go home] and just before it pulled off, Bill Dellinger came up to me and said, 'Do you know why I choose you?'

I said, "'No, why? Why won't you let me out of my commitment?'"

Bill replied, 'Because I knew you weren't a quitter.'

"I think that if he had challenged me and told me to get my butt back out to practice, I would've left. But basically he was saying that 'You are better than that.'"

The bond of athlete and coach formed between Mack and Dellinger would bring David to a whole other level of his running, and it would be a bond that remained well beyond David's collegiate career. In the spring of 2018, when John Truax began a documentary project on the legendary Coach Dellinger, Bill was asked which of his Duck athletes he wanted to be sure that would be included in the film. He responded without hesitation that David Mack needed to be included.

For many college freshmen that first year on your own can be tough to adjust to. For NCAA division 1 athletes, the transition is even more pronounced. The rigors of a higher level of training, being on your own for the first time, and all the temptations that this independence provides can bring about the demise of many first year athletes. The Ducks would lose one of the top distance recruits, Jeff Nelson, who would return to Southern California to continue his education at Glendale Community College after his fall semester. When asked about David's ability to make such a successful transition from high school to college, the question of David's independence that he developed taking care of himself from his early childhood, Coach Dellinger acknowledged that this certainly played an important part of David's success.

In addition to the transition to college life as an NCAA D-1 athlete, David also had to deal with the transition of coming from Compton, California to Eugene, Oregon. Teammate Greg Erwin's earlier observation about David being a fish out of water is insightful when looking at how David's upbringing caused some trouble for him early on. David recalls an incident at a Eugene McDonalds before school had even started. "When you're raised a certain way the survival instinct is always present. I've always felt that colleges recruit kids from the inner city, the ghetto, the barrio, or the trailer park, and they need to understand that when you recruit these kids their life skills that they have to survive with are totally different from and don't translate over to college life. You see these [college] kids getting into trouble, and no one had the foresight to say, 'Hey, we've got to help these kids transition.' For the people from the outside, they just read their papers and say, 'Look at that stupid kid. He had a chance of a lifetime and screwed it up.'

Well, who taught him? They didn't know any better. They [the recruiting colleges] only picked them for their athletic ability. They don't understand that growing up in these environments is very hostile. I got into it with two guys in McDonald's before school ever started. I was up to throwing down with two guys, and the manager called the police. These were my life survival skills where I escalated something that wasn't a threat. From the environment I had come from, it was a threat. These two guys were looking at me, so in my environment in the hood if someone is staring at you, you've got to address that; it's a personal challenge. Since there were two of them, they're like, 'Fuck you! Fuck you!' and it's on all because of what I had perceived in my head. Had I just ignored it and gone on about my business nothing would have happened. Those are the residual effects of growing up in the inner city. Those are the survival skills that helped me to survive, but those are not the skills needed to have a positive experience on a university campus."

David looked forward to being teammates with rival Jeff West at U of O

31

David Mack finds the only thing to like about Eugene is Bill Dellinger; the Oregon coach finds many things to like about his freshman runner

A well worn and beloved 1979 Eugene Register Guard photo of David and Coach Dellinger

Chapter 6
A Successful Rookie Season

With the bond between coach and athlete forged, David began his preparation for his freshman year at the University of Oregon in earnest. With his early arrival on campus, and his reputation that had preceded him, David was quite the anomaly on the Eugene campus. Life in Oregon was certainly different from life in South Central L.A.. Fellow freshman recruit and teammate, Jim Hill, recalls a story of one of their first runs together. "David and I were running up around Mt. Pisgah and some hunters were shooting off in the distance. David hits the ground and is yelling at me to hit the ground too. Growing up on the edge of suburbia and the country in Virginia, I didn't think too much about it, but from where David was from the sound of gunshots had an entirely different association." David and Jim would forge a decades long friendship over many miles run together and stay in contact still to this day.

It came as a bit of surprise to David when he attended the fall training camp in the Cascades Mountains of Oregon with the cross country team members. While David had run cross country at Locke High School in Los Angeles, he was now surrounded by one of the greatest collections of collegiate distance talent in the US. Joining XC All-American Duck team members Alberto Salazar (9th), Don Clary (12th), Rudy Chapa (27th), and Billy McChesney (28th) of the 1977 NCAA XC champion team during the fall of David's first year would be incoming freshman standouts US high school national record holder, Jeff Nelson of Burbank High School in Southern California and Jim Hill of Oakton, Virginia.

The Ducks, loaded with even more talent, would finish second to the University of Texas at El Paso in the 1979 NCAA XC Championship meet. The Miners of UTEP had beaten the Ducks the previous year 56-72 (lowest score wins) behind all-American finishes of Salazar (1st), Clary (7th), Chapa (14th) and Ken Martin (17th). The 1979 team chopped that deficit of sixteen points down to seven points.

While David did not race fall cross country, he held his own with these Men Of Oregon on distance runs as he built his base for the spring season. Sophomore teammate, Greg Erwin, recalls the annual pre-season cross country camp at Odell Lake near the Willamette Pass in the Cascades that

Coach Dellinger took the team to. He included David among the dozen harriers on this trip. The 4,800 foot elevation and forest covered trails would be an entirely different training environment than what David was used to. Erwin was asked by Coach Dellinger to take the new recruits Jeff Nelson, Jim Hill, and David on an easy morning run of five to seven miles in the forest around Odell Lake. "As often happened, our easy run turned into a fast run. Jim and I decided to add on another mile or so up into the mountain and then turn back to meet up with everyone else. We're moving along, and Jim is running faster and faster along these little forest roads. I figured everyone else had turned around by now, but then I heard someone else behind us. It's David, and he's got this real determined look on his face. So we're running along at this real aggressive pace — probably around 5:30 a mile — at elevation on these forest covered trails. I've told Jim looking back on that now, and I have to wonder if that was determination or pure terror. This was a kid who had probably never seen so many trees in his life and had certainly, probably, never been in the forest before. Here was an 800 meter guy hanging with two 5k/10k guys who were running pretty hard, uphill, at altitude."

David impressed his teammates that day and not because he was trying to earn a spot on the fall cross country team, but simply because he demonstrated that when presented with a challenge, he was one that would not back down. This fearlessness became a trademark of David's racing, and it would show itself on training runs at various times. Erwin recollects a story from a warm September training run with David, Jeff Nelson, and Jim Hill on Pre's Trails across the Willamette River from campus, "David and Jeff wanted to stop on the [Autzen] footbridge to watch some of the people floating the river in inner tubes and rafts. Nelson and Mack begin taking their shoes off and climbing up on the rail getting ready to jump. I'm screaming at these guys, 'You're crazy! You can't do that! The water isn't deep enough!' Before any of us could do anything, Mack jumps off in that rapidly moving water."

Being late in the summer, the river was quite low, but David jumped in regardless. Fortunately, he hit the water where it was deep enough but he went under. Greg recalls, "Jim and I ran to the other side of the bridge so that we could get close to the shore. We're waiting, waiting, waiting, and I'm like 'Oh my God' because he's still underwater. Finally, his head pops up and he cranes his neck, gasping for air, and the river is just pushing him down with no control over anything. Nelson had jumped in around the same time just after him. Both of these knotheads are struggling to get out of the water. Jim and I get down to the bank, and I'm yelling at them because as a sophomore and a year older, I knew that Dellinger would kill me if something had happened to these two recruits." Fortunately for Greg, Jim, and David, when Dellinger was reminded of this incident, all he would do was chuckle and shake his head.

Since 1980 was an Olympic year, Dellinger had redshirted his veterans Alberto Salazar and Rudy Chapa to prepare for the Moscow Games, so the Ducks were without these veterans for leadership. In their absence, David soon filled that role both on the team and for the fans. Erwin recalls, "David was an immediate fan favorite at Hayward. He had a fearless racing style, and he never backed down from anybody. Whether it was the 800 meters where he was unbeatable, or the occasional 1500 meter, or the 4x400 relay, where he was 'Golden', the fans loved him."

Hayward Field fans got to see him race quite a bit that first year; the Oregon Invitational meet, the Kansas dual meet, the Indiana dual meet, the WSU dual meet, the Oregon Twilight Invitational, and finally at the Olympic Trials.

While many appreciated the successes of David on the track, few could understand what he went through off the track. "It was a culture shock for me," says David. "It was tough making that transition; I think it's even tougher for kids who are a big fish in a little pond. Now if you are just a little guppy here with the names Pre, Salazar, Chapa, and McChesney all around you, you've got to find your own way. And I did."

It wasn't just running in the shadows of legends either that contributed to this difficult transition. "I was a really marginal student, so I had to apply myself because I had such learning issues. I had a late start in education, so I had to spend many nights in my dorm studying just to get Cs. Coach Dellinger instilled in me a great deal of discipline."

Dellinger, himself a three time Olympian and bronze medalist in the 1964 Tokyo 5000 meters, an American and World record holder, and NCAA and conference champion, had been coached by the legendary Bill Bowerman. Dellinger would take over the head coaching position from Bowerman in 1972 and garnered tremendous success. Named Track and Field Pac-10 Coach of the Year five times and Cross Country Pac-10 Coach of the Year twelve times, Dellinger knew how to get the best out of his runners.

David thrived under Dellinger's coaching. David would earn his first of three Pac-10 800 meter titles at the University of Washington running 1:48.28 defeating friend and rival Jeff West of UCLA, who finished second. The Bruins would flip the score in the team competition winning 163-116 over the Ducks.

David's impact was not just seen on the scoreboard but on his teammates as well. One fellow Duck sprinter, Bart MacGillivray recalls with fondness the camaraderie that existed between David and him, "He always went out of his way to include me. Running on the University of Oregon team was extremely competitive day in and day out in workouts. You were fighting for your position on the team. He was a compassionate, caring guy along with that side of intensity. One evening I was beat up after practice. I was worn out, and he could sense that I was struggling a bit, and David just took it upon himself to share a poem that his high school coach [Coach Don Strametz] had given him. The poem was titled "It's All in the State of Mind". One of the first things that I reminded David of when we reconnected a few years ago was that poem. It was that impactful. David had that capacity with me to really understand the challenges."

It's All In the State of Mind
By Walter D. Wintle
If you think you are beaten, you are,
If you think that you dare not, you don't,
If you'd like to win, but you think you can't,
It's almost certain you won't.
If you think you'll lose, you've lost,
For out in the world you'll find
Success begins with a fellow's will—Full many a race is lost
Ere even a step is run,
And many a coward falls
Ere even his work's begun,
Think big, and your deeds will grow;
Think small, and you'll fall behind;
Think that you can, and you will—
It's all in the state of mind.

If you think you are outclassed, you are;
You've got to think high to rise;
You've got to be sure of yourself before
You ever can win a prize,
Life's battles don't always go
To the stronger or faster man;
But soon or late the man who wins
Is the man who thinks he can.

David had read this poem, given to him by Coach Strametz, before every big race during his high school career, and now he had paid it forward to his freshman year teammate. A simple act of friendship with a heartfelt impact; from coach to athlete, from athlete to teammate. Many of us never realize the profound influence our simple actions have on those around us.

The Ducks rested their 1980 NCAA championship hopes on the strength of a relatively small contingent. All-American performances by Tom Hinthaus (2nd in Pole Vault), Ken Martin (2nd in Steeplechase), Billy McChesney (3rd in 5000m), Jon Switzer (5th in PV) and David's sixth place in the 800 meters would be solid enough for sixth place in the team scoring.

Even with the surprise sixth place finish, David was not satisfied and had expected more. "I was so dejected because I didn't win. I was a winner! Just because it was my first year in college doesn't mean I'm not supposed to win. I had my head down, and the first person to come up to me was [5000 meter All-American teammate] Billy McChesney. He said, 'Keep your head up; you did great. You have nothing to be ashamed of.' I didn't take it well then, but I'll never forget his encouragement. Then Bill Dellinger found me in the tunnel with my head down, and he said, 'Hey, great job!' I looked at him, 'Are you crazy?' And he told me, 'You did great. I'm so proud of you; hold your head up.' And these are the things you learn and remember throughout your life. People coming to your side."

Despite a U.S.A. boycott of the 1980 Moscow Olympics, David used his successful collegiate season to ready himself for the Olympic Trials meet which was held on his home Hayward Field's Stevenson Track. In the opening prelims round David found himself in the same heat as Jeff West. West won the heat in 1:48.08, but David qualified for the semifinals with his third place finish (1:48.41).

David sent a message to the veterans in his semi-final round winning in 1:47.02 over Randy Wilson, James Robinson, Johnny Gray, and West, who would be eliminated. The veterans would not be complacent and disregard David in the finals. Despite Mark Enyeart's opening 400 meter split of 51.8, the Hayward fans clapped and stomped for David to hang on, but Villanova NCAA champion, Don Paige, would run negative splits of 52.3 and 52.2 to win in 1:44.53. Former Cal Berkeley sensation, James Robinson would finish second, and Randy Wilson of Athletes In Action would round out the top three. It would take a lifetime best of 1:46.67 for David to equal his NCAA sixth place finish. David would place ahead of former Crenshaw High School rival, Johnny Gray. This was not their first race against each other, nor would this be their last. Gray, Mack, and West would eventually run together the following summer for the Santa Monica Track Club.

Following his successful debut season, one would think that David would be on a plane to Europe for the summer. Unfortunately, in 1980 professionalism in track & field was just dawning. David, without a coach or manager for that summer, returned home to South Central L.A. and spent his time training himself preparing for his upcoming sophomore season. He still feels a sense of bitterness knowing that he was bypassed by the TAC (The Athletics Congress) for the summer University Games simply because the officials wrongfully assumed that after the season that David had that he would most assuredly be on the European circuit. "It was like a slap in the face. I'd run for the University of Oregon. I had qualified, but I didn't have Joe Douglas as a manager. I didn't know anyone. My season ended right after the Olympic Trials."

David's first race at Hayward Field, the lead-off leg (1200m) of the DMR at
the Oregon Invitational. Here he is racing against
Athletics West's Phil "Tiny" Kane.

David's winning effort as anchor for the Duck's 4x4 relay

David would place 3rd in 4:04.29 at the Oregon Twilight Mile behind Matt Centrowitz (not pictured) and Chris Horton.

David did it all for the Ducks running an occasional 1500 meters but dominating in the 800 meters and mile relay.

David and teammate Parrish Nixon get ready for the 4x4 relay.

**David wins his Olympic Trials semi final sending a message to
Dan Futrell (141), Jeff West, Johnny Gray (162), and Randy Wilson (484).
James Robinson (not pictured) would finish third at 1:47.38
and qualify for the finals**

.

Chapter 7
'81 and '82 Seasons:
Two More Pac-10 Titles and an NCAA Title

After his successful debut season at the University of Oregon, David demonstrated that he was ready for even more. No longer a freshman, David became a legend in the making at Hayward Field. Greg Erwin describes this growth in David, "I have always said that David was perhaps the greatest athlete, in terms of range, ever at the U of O. He ran an occasional 1500 meter, but I think he could have stepped up and become a successful 5000 meter runner. Number one: he was fearless. Number two: he had a talent that he could run anywhere from 45.6 for the 400 meter, and he probably could have run a 3:54 mile at that time. To me he was one of the physically greatest talents that I'd ever seen for sure during my time at U of O, and perhaps even of all runners I've seen. A lot of guys who have a great deal of talent when they're young didn't work hard. I always remember David as being a hard worker; he trained hard and did everything he was supposed to do."

When asked nearly forty years after his time at University of Oregon about his impact as a Duck, David jokes, "Prefontaine might have been the most famous, but I guess I might be the most infamous."

David's work ethic became his expectation for others. As Gary Kelly, his teammate from Locke High School said, "David took it personally when his teammates didn't give their very best." This became evident to freshman hurdler, Don Ward, a recruit to the University of Oregon out of the Bay area. Don had seen David run in 1979 at the state meet and welcomed the chance to be on the Ducks team with him. Don became a hurdler during his junior year after being on the baseball team his ninth and tenth grade years. Track came easy to him, and his successes came without much effort. One day at practice, David pulled Don aside, "He ripped into me one day. He got on me. 'You're wasting a bunch of talent. You don't understand what it takes. Everything comes easy for you.' And this was in both track and in school. I kind of discounted it at the time, but after I got older and more mature, I saw what he was trying to do for me and reach out to me. He wanted me to understand that if I put more effort into things, I could do a lot more with my life. I've learned over life that 'Time is Cruel' because sometimes the message that we get, we are not ready for it."

David demonstrated his talent and work ethic as he repeated as Pac-10 800 meter champion his sophomore year this time at Stanford University running 1:46.99 and again defeating friend and rival Jeff West. The Ducks would again place second in the Pac-10 this time behind Arizona State University 133-114 on the shoulders of first place finishes by Mack, Alberto Salazar (5k & 10k), and Reidar Lorentzen (Javelin).

At the NCAA championships that year, David qualified in the 800 meters. Unfortunately, he ran poorly in the prelims and did not advance to the finals. The Ducks team would finish a disappointing tie for eleventh place with Baylor, Georgia, and Northwestern State with a mere 16 points. He attributed his disappointing race to a combination of coming down with strep throat, a severe case of shin splints and compounding that by running a tactically bad race.

Another instance of David's frustration with him not accepting anything but the best from others came during the Pac-10 Championships at Stanford University his sophomore year. Don remembers that David had become frustrated with the coaches' decision to run David, another half miler, a 200 meter runner, and himself in the 4x400 relay, "I ran third leg and Mack ran anchor. He was so pissed off that we got paired with these guys that when we got over to the warmup track, he was mumbling. We ended up making it to the next round, and he says, 'I'm not running with those guys.' He ran a 45.6 and I ran a 45.8 and we ended up bringing the team back."

David followed up his sophomore season as a Duck with an outstanding European season. He ran a PR of 1:46.03 behind James Robinson (1:45.53), Mike Boit of Kenya (1:45.60) and Randy Wilson (1:45.82) in the 800 meters at the TAC Championship meet in Sacramento that summer of 1981, and then proceeded to run in Europe with the Santa Monica Track Club. He finished the season as the # 4 ranked 800 meter runner of the US by *Track and Field News*.

Having won two Pac-10 800 meter titles and earning All-American status as a freshman but failing to improve in the NCAA meet his sophomore year gave David motivation to make his junior year at U of O even better. Once again David held to his long-held belief, "In life you have to find reasons to succeed and not fail."

Perhaps the fire that fueled David's drive stemmed from his difficult and dangerous life as a child where he essentially raised himself. Perhaps it came from his desire to make something more of his life than he had growing up in Compton. Whatever the motivation behind his drive, it always manifested itself in his races. David ran like he lived; the tougher the fight the tougher he ran. This was never more evident than in a seemingly inconsequential dual meet against WSU at Hayward Field his junior year. In the WSU dual meet the previous year, he and rival Cougar half miler, Sotirios Moutsauas, had battled for the precious second and third place points at Pullman with David, who had battled shin splints all season, came up on the short end of this match-up. In their race during David's junior year, David had not forgotten the previous year's race. David ran an easy pace in first place to assist a teammate, Chris Hudson, in staying close so that they might go 1-2. When David turned around mid-race to call his teammate urging him to keep up, Moutsauas, the Greek 800 meter record holder, took offense thinking that David was ridiculing him. Sotirios surged and even passed David during the final lap, giving David an elbow to lay down the gauntlet. David responded immediately and ran away from the mad Greek half miler gaining the victory in 1:50.11. "After the race, Moutsauas came up to me to say something, and I pushed him away." Each race, even a dual meet with just four runners on a wet and cold April afternoon in front of the Hayward faithful became a battle for David. He attributes this fire to his hard life growing up, "I'm not making any excuses, but I grew up in a hostile, violent climate, and when someone threatens you or hurts you, you didn't negotiate. You immediately struck back and with hopefully more force than with what they came at you with to subdue them."

His final season as a Duck allowed David to go out in a big way. He won his third Pac-10 800 meter title in front of the Hayward fans in 1:48.11 over Pete Richardson of ASU. The Ducks' team finished fourth (80.5 points) as a team behind UCLA (146 points), WSU (113 points), and Arizona State (113 points).

Whereas the Duck runners could acclimate for the 1980 and 1981 NCAA championships by wearing extra sweats and rainsuits to simulate the heat and humidity of Austin, Texas and Baton Rouge, Louisiana, the 1982 championships meet would be contested at an altitude of 4,553 feet at BYU in Provo, Utah. The rarified air at that altitude would be a distinct disadvantage for any school coming up from lower elevations. Not to be deterred, David would earn an NCAA title along with throwers Dean Crouser (Shot Put and

Discus) and Brian Crouser (Javelin), and their first place finishes along with other Duck All-Americans Jim Hill (5th in the 1500m) and Billy McChesney (5th in the 5000 meters) would secure a fourth place trophy for the Ducks. David became the second half miler in U of O history, behind Wade Bell of the 1967 team, to earn an NCAA title in that event. Three other Ducks have done it since David's time; Joaquim Cruz ('83 & '84); Andrew Wheating ('09 & '10); and Elijah Greer ('13). Mack finished his career (1:45.55) as the # 2 all-time Duck 800 meter runner behind Wade Bell (1:45.17). [Since his time there, he has been overtaken by Joaquim Cruz (1:41.77), Andrew Wheating (1:45.03), and Elijah Greer (1:45.06)].

David looked at his future and realized that with his NCAA title, he had achieved all that he could as a collegian. Ever since his successful high school and freshman collegiate years, he had wondered about the possibility of running professionally. He saw that running might very well be his way to making some money as he heard about the changing tide of runners being paid to compete and receive money from shoe companies to wear their gear. Professional running, still in its infancy, meant that David would have to capitalize on that limited window of opportunity.

David recalls that first professional contract, "When I first signed with Nike, I made quite a bit. That was a big difference from being in the dorms and being on a scholarship. And it was guaranteed for three years. [Looking back compared to now] The money wasn't big because we were just transitioning [into professional track and field contracts]. It was a 'golden age' to have a manager like Joe Douglas, who was looking out for his athletes for the first time whereas before athletes were being taken advantage of."

David pauses during his pre-race prep to watch his girlfriend, Florence Griffith, getting ready to run the 4x100 for UCLA at the 1981 U of O vs. Auburn/UCLA dual meet.

Feeling at home in Eugene… finally.

David earned three Pac-10 800 meter titles and an NCAA title as well.

David settles in at the finals of the NCAA 800 meter finals

David finishes his collegiate career with an NCAA title

Chapter 8
Time To Go Back Home

Having accomplished all that he could and still struggling with the academics of college life, David decided to take a chance at his shot as a professional track athlete. "I was pretty naive then. Nike was always talking to me. 'You know, you should just leave the University of Oregon and come run professionally. You've accomplished everything,' and I was really struggling financially and academically. So I just said, 'I'm out of here.' Nike dangling the money at me was not just so much about the money, but it was also about me being poor. Here was my opportunity. This gave me a sense of security."

Duck teammate, Jim Hill, remembers that during "Dead Week" he had bumped into David outside of Mac Court and asked him about his preparation for finals next week. David indicated that he wasn't going to bother taking them as he saw himself as already being done. His time as a Duck being finished, he now turned his attention to the summer European season.

Coach Dellinger has acknowledged that he harbored no ill will towards David's decision to leave a year early. He knew what that money would mean to him as a young athlete. David's decision to turn pro before graduating, although the norm for many NCAA basketball and football athletes these days, was relatively unheard of in the early 80s. He would tell *Track and Field News*, "The thing I really regret is not going for four [Pac 10 titles] in a row and the [Hayward Field] crowds."

David would also miss his relationship with Coach Dellinger. Though some thirty-five years removed from his time being coached by Bill, he stays in contact and has visited him every time he gets up to Eugene. "Even though Bill can't verbalize it as well these days [after a stroke in the summer of 2000], you can see it in his eyes, read it in his body language, and sense the enthusiasm of what he wants to say. You can see the frustration he's experiencing because he can't get it out."

David joined Santa Monica Track Club teammates and coach, Joe Douglas after leaving Eugene. His introduction into post collegiate running was a rough one. In his semi-final heat of the TAC National Championships meet at Knoxville, Tennessee a week after his NCAA victory, he found himself boxed in on the inside rail. "I wasn't used to this aggressive running because many of these guys [his 800 meter competitors] were from the boards [indoors racing]. He [Bill Martin] saw me; he looked at me in the eye, and he just leaned over into me. He came over to cut me off and spiked me. I felt it; I looked and saw the blood squirt from my quad. I just ran up alongside him and slapped all the sparks out of the side of his face. I smacked him, and then I won my heat. I went up and told Joe [Douglas], 'You might want to go check with the official. I think I might get disqualified.'"

Confrontations such as the ones with WSU's Sotirios Moutsauas and Athletic West's Bill Martin would prepare David for the aggressive running of Europe. No longer a collegian, and now on the world stage, David competed throughout Europe. SMTC teammate Johnny Gray observes, "This was a time [in the early days of "professional running"] when many Americans weren't traveling overseas. We were two of the few Americans over there, and we had a lot of fun. Joe Douglas had a track club that really guided us, took care of us, and kept us focused. It was because of this that we were able to reach the levels that we reached."

Coach Douglas soon realized that it would be best for Mack and Gray's development to not always run them in the same meets. So he carefully crafted their race schedules to race on opposite days or opposite meets. Gray explains, "Joe said, 'You guys when you are running together are just killing each other,' because we were trying to compete with each other, and we wouldn't focus the right way [on the other competitors]. So we would go to different meets, and if I would run a PR, he [David] would hear about it, and then he would run a PR and beat my time. Back and forth trying to outdo one another. It was fun."

Not every day was spent racing and training though. As twenty-somethings traveling throughout Europe, Johnny and David also found time for sightseeing. One such excursion occurred in Lausanne, Switzerland. Looking to stay off their feet as much as possible they decided to go down to the public beach along the river, which flowed into Lake Geneva. When they got there, they soon realized that in Europe it was not uncommon for the people to swim and sunbathe in the nude. So as the old saying goes, "When in Lausanne…." Johnny picks up the story after the two had followed the custom of the locals and had decided to swim, "We were a little uncomfortable because we were the only ones fully dressed. We took our clothes off and got in the water at an area that looked like it was easy to swim in. The current took us down and we almost lost our lives. It took us at least a mile out, and it was only because of our fitness that we survived it. If it wasn't for the shape that we were in, we would've drowned. We got scarred up by the rocks, but luckily on the side I got hold of a branch and was able to hold on and try to recover. I pulled myself to the shore but I was naked. We are quite far away from our clothes, but now I'm worried about David. I found something to cover myself up with, and I started running down [the shore line] hollering for David. I finally heard him, and he's on the side holding a branch trying to recover. He pulled himself out and found something to cover himself up with. Then we had to walk back to where our clothes were. That was an experience."

Aside from his marathon swim session to save his life, David's best performance of his debut professional season would be a third place at the Bislett Games 800 meters in Oslo, Norway in 1:45.55 behind Garry Cook of Great Britain (1:44.71) and James Robinson (1:44.72).

He finished the 1982 season ranked # 4 in the *Track and Field News* US rankings behind: 1) James Robinson; 2) Steve Scott; and 3) Johnny Gray. Few, except for perhaps David, could have anticipated what a breakout season his next year would be.

Of all the things David would miss most in leaving U of O in 1982, the Hayward Field crowd would hold a special place in his heart.

Almost three decades after their time together as athlete and coach, David and Coach Dellinger reminisce over their relationship.

**David would find the transition to professional running rough at first.
He would get DQ'd in his 1982 TAC semi-final for retaliating against
Athletic West's Bill Martin.**

Chapter 9
Santa Monica Track Club and the Amazing '83 Season

The inaugural IAAF World Championships were introduced in 1983 providing track and field athletes with a world championship event every four years in the year preceding the Olympics. The 1983 World Championship meet, held in Helsinki, Finland gave David the chance to gain international experience in a championship meet format (prelims/semi finals/finals).

David had qualified for the '83 team in the 800 meters by finishing second in a PR of 1:44.78 along with James Robinson (1st) and David Patrick (3rd) at the June TAC championship meet in Indianapolis. In his pre-World Championship European races, he would get a taste of the aggressive style of racing that he had limited exposure to back in the states, "I was not used to the aggressive running in Europe. They're is a lot of elbowing and pushing that if you did that in the States, you'd get disqualified for that. That's how it is over there, and I wasn't used to it. Willi Wülbeck [of West Germany] got into a shoving match in Luxembourg [July 20th], and I pushed the shit out of him. I had fingernails, and he ended up with scars on his shoulder. David would finish 3rd behind James Robinson of the USA (1:44.32) and Joaquim Cruz of Brazil (1:45.00).

In the preliminary rounds of the World Championships in Helsinki on August 7th, David ran a tactical race to win in 1:45.84 over Jorma Härkonen (1:46.39) of Finland. On the next day, running in a semifinals race with Willi Wülbeck (1:46.26) of West Germany, Agberto Guimares (1:46.37) of Brazil, Jose Marajo (1:46.39) of France, David would also run 1:46.39 and miss making the finals by two one-hundredths of a second. Wülbeck would go on to win the finals in 1:43.65.

Living by the motto of always trying to find and focus on the reasons to succeed and not the excuse to fail, David put together one of the most amazing seasons in American track and field. His failure to advance to the finals in Helsinki would motivate him to run with purpose for the remainder of the European season.

According to an article by Jon Hendershott of *Track and Field News* "[SMTC coach Joe Douglas said] 'We felt that David was ready for a very fast time, and a couple of days after the WC final, I gave him a 500 meter time trial in training. I wanted him to run the first 400 in 49-- so he ran 47.4 and

58.9 for the 500. He took a two lap jog and then did a 48.8 400. He jogged another 2 laps and then did a 200 under 22 seconds. So that was a good indicator that he was in great condition.'"

What David would accomplish over the next three weeks of August and the first week of September would go down in the history of track and field as some of the finest running ever witnessed. On Wednesday August 17th, David traveled to West Berlin for the ISATF meet, where he would be booed by the German fans because of the scuffle that he and Willi Wülbeck got into in Luxembourg. He would win in a PR of 1:44.73. This was followed by another win the next Wednesday in Zurich, Switzerland at the Weltklasse meet. His time in Zurich was 1:44.62, another PR. On Friday the 26th he placed fourth behind World Championships silver medalist Rob Druppers of the Netherlands (1:44.90) and Steve Ovett (1:45.25). David's time of 1:45.33 would have been a lifetime best aside from his earlier three sub 1:45 times of this season.

Two days later, David was asked to rabbit a 1500 meter World Record attempt by Sydney Maree at a meet in Cologne, West Germany. German quarter miler, Bernard Knocke, took the pack out in 54.7 for the first 400 meters. When Knocke peeled off, David took over pacing duties and brought Maree through 800 meters in 1:52.8. In a *Track and Field News* article on the race it said, "Mack set a brisk tempo, periodically turning to shout encouragement to Maree. 'He was making fun of me a little' revealed the Villanova grad. 'Before the race, I told him to go hard, go hard, so he kept saying to me, 'C'mon, Sydney. C'mon.'"

David had brought out the best in Sydney with his pace setting and encouragement and helped Maree break Englishman Steve Ovett's three year old record. Maree's time 3:31.24 would last just seven days as Ovett would set out to reclaim his record in Rieti, Italy.

David capitalized on his fitness by notching another win and another sub-1:45 800 meter time, his fourth of the season, at Koblenz, Germany. His time of 1:44.39 was not only a lifetime PR, but it also made him only the second person in US track and field history to run four sub 1:45 times in a season; only Rick Wolhuter had accomplished the same honor in the 1974 season. The rabbit in his Koblenz race had taken the pace out at 50.1, which according to David in a *Track and Field News* article, "That was a little too fast. I think if I had gone through in something like 50.8 I would have run faster; maybe even breaking the American Record."

The very next day, Mack traveled to Rome for yet another victory; this time in a 1:45.79. From Rome, David would make the 45 mile trip to Rietti three days later to perform pacing duties for Steve Ovett's world record attempt. He had been successful in being the rabbit for Sydney Maree's world record, and he was fit. Now some might think disparaging things about those runners hired to run only a portion of the race, but David was not bothered. In a *Track and Field News* article David said, "I don't understand the stereotype with rabbiting. You're supposed to be insulted, but I wasn't. I thought it was fun."

Despite terribly windy conditions, David took his job seriously and did it quite well. He led Ovett through laps of 54.2 (400 meters) and 1:51.7 (800 meters) more than a second faster than he had been in Maree's world record race seven days earlier. Ovett praised Mack's pacing in the same *T&F News* article. "He was a fantastic pacemaker and his effort was 60% of the race," said Ovett. "A good pacemaker allows you to relax mentally and physically. He's like the Columbia Space Shuttle; the rocket takes you so far and then you have to shoot for the moon. I just gave it hell from there- but I was surprised when I saw I had broken the record."

Almost 6100 miles away, David's high school coach, Tony Yeoman, happened to see David's race on TV while waiting in line to rent a movie at a Blockbuster in Northern California. Yeoman suspected that David had more in the tank, "David's setting the pace, and there he is at the 1100 meter mark, right on the pace [for the WR], and he looked so good that as he was stepping off the track, I didn't know why David Mack didn't continue to go along with him and finish the race. I think he could have been right there. Oh, my gosh, I had no idea that he was running. I just happened to walk right in there to rent a movie, and there he was running."

For all intents and purposes, it appeared that David's decision to turn professional was a good one. *Track and Field News* rewarded Mack's season in the end of year rankings; # 1 in the US and # 3 in the world. Nike would reward David's efforts with bonuses. Perhaps even more significant for David was the cadre of teammates that he became surrounded by. Having grown up in his early childhood without much of any family, David sought surrogate family connections. Throughout David's life he became the best person that he could be when he was surrounded by those that provided him with love and support. One could argue that the track teams that David became a part of at Locke High School, at the University of Oregon, and at Santa Monica Track Club filled that void from his early childhood. Additionally, coach Joe Douglas would set out to provide David with not just world class coaching and management, but he would play the role of a father figure for him that would last for decades to come. Despite David being a 20 year old, grown man, Joe still felt the need to check on him at night while traveling between meet to meet throughout Europe to make sure David would get the needed sleep to compete at the highest level in the next day's race. While recounting meet results from David's races in Europe, nearly forty years later, Joe can recall those results that were not reflective of David's best due to late nights past curfew. Listening to Joe recount stories of David's races, a palpable sense of a father-like pride permeates his telling.

David would make it to the semifinals of the inaugural World Championships meet in Helsinki

David runs his PR of 1:44.39 at Koblenz.

David worked as the pacemaker for two world records. He paced Steve Ovett
through 1100 meters to break Sydney Maree's week old 1500 meter WR, which
David had also rabitted.

Chapter 10
A Nike Deal "From Stealing Shoes
to Being Paid to Wear Their Shoes"

David's successful '83 season meant more fame and notoriety. He found himself in the company of not just Olympians and World Record holders like Carl Lewis and Steve Ovett, but also Hollywood celebrities like George Burns and Debbie Allen. For some, that kind of a rise to fame can go to a young athlete's head. For David it caused him to pause and reflect on the irony of his life as it had unfolded to this point, "I can remember telling my wife when I signed my first Nike contract, I had tears in my eyes because I used to steal shoes in Compton. I was banned from stores because I was always stealing their shoes. So in the irony of life, here's someone paying me to wear their shoes. My life has a lot of twists and turns."

The transition from stealing shoes in Compton to a Nike sponsored athlete came about with the assistance of coach, manager, and mentor, Joe Douglas. Joe takes pride in his approach to promoting the sport of track and field in general and his athletes in particular. "What I tried to do with my athletes in Europe, if they had been running well I'd try to get them interviewed two or three days before the meet when we got there, so they could get their picture in the paper; that's the reason Carl Lewis made so much money. They'd always interview him, and then we could fill up the stadium. These interviews would give publicity to the athlete, to the Santa Monica Track Club, to the meet, and to track and field altogether." Joe explains that this was no coincidence, "According to the meet director at Zurich, they'd had 5000 to 6000 tickets sold prior to the team's arrival for the meet. Once my guys rolled in and started appearing on the news and the papers ticket sales soard. We filled that 46,000 seat stadium."

David's fame reached a pinnacle when Nike featured him in a prominent Clio Award winning advertising campaign in the build-up to the 1984 L.A. Olympics. An image of a post-workout, contemplative David featuring Nike shoes and clothes with his own shadow looming over his shoulder on the wall behind him would appear in *Rolling Stone* and *GQ Magazines*, on Nike posters, and on 100 foot by 50 foot billboards all around Southern California. "It was 1984 and I was big time. I was getting ready for the Olympics, and they sent a limo over to pick me up. I had just come off a great season, and I was third in the world. I was picked to win the silver medal at the L.A. Olympics."

That image of the shadow looming over his shoulder might be seen as a harbinger of what was to come, as, unfortunately, sometimes life doesn't always go the way you were hoping.

Expectations were high for David going into the '84 Games in LA.

Chapter 11
Injury in '84 Ends Olympic Dream

The shin splints that plagued David during his 1981 season flared up once again during his '84 season. Unfortunately, instead of it just being shin splints his injury became diagnosed as compartment syndrome, which is a painful condition that occurs when pressure within the muscles builds to a debilitating degree. This pressure can decrease blood flow, which prevents nourishment and oxygen from reaching nerve and muscle cells. David grew accustomed to dealing with the pain, "When I used to get out of the bed in the morning, it was just an absolute nightmare. I would just sit on the floor."

David ran some races in the early portion of the 1984 build-up to the Olympics, but his performances were nowhere near what he had accomplished the previous year. At the TAC Championships in San Jose in early June, he struggled to a 7th place finish in 1:49.21. Ten days later, David would toe the line at the Olympic Trials in the L.A. Coliseum. He ran fast enough to qualify and made it through the prelims with his 4th place finish in a lackluster 1:49.21. His legs would not tolerate the pain the next day in the quarter finals though, where he finished 8th in a pedestrian 1:56.01. Running with compartment syndrome is painful; racing at an international level becomes impossible. For David, it would mean an end to his 1984 Olympic dream. The loss of the chance to run at the L.A. Coliseum on the world stage, just a few miles from where he grew up, might have been even more painful than the injury and the surgery that would follow.

Once again as things looked the bleakest in David's life, he needed an angel. Coach Joe Douglas recommended that David see Houston orthopedic surgeon, Dr. Don Baxter, who served as an unofficial team doctor for the Santa Monica Track Club, and would be just that angel for David. Dr. Baxter had been a part of the first running boom of the early 70s performing one of the earliest compartment syndrome surgeries on Steve Prefontaine's 1972 Olympic teammate, Leonard Hilton, where he released a nerve in his heel — a hindfoot compartment. Dr. Baxter would perform the necessary surgery on both of David's legs on July 4th, which proved to be David's independence [from pain] day.

Dr. Baxter, having been a track and field athlete himself — 400 meters, high jump, and decathlon in high school and college — had a special place in his heart for David and all the athletes he's worked on. He knows what it is to compete and values the benefits that a life of exercise can provide. Dr. Baxter ran his first marathon in 1972 at age 29 and is able to boast of having run a marathon in each decade for six decades having completed his most recent a few years ago at Boston at age 70.

David's successful surgery of his deep posterior medial compartment would give him another chance at pursuing his running goals. According to Dr. Baxter, "The tibial nerve was being entrapped by the deep muscles. All I had to do was make an incision five to six inches along the medial side of his leg. I got down to the deep fascia and released the pressure off the tibial nerve." Dr. Baxter told David after the surgery, "Usually when I cut the sheath, the muscle just oozes out, but when I cut his it just popped out."

Dr. Baxter reflects on the role that he played not only in David's life but in all the athletes' lives that he's performed surgery on, "Renowned orthopedic trauma surgeon, Sig Hansen, once told me, 'With sports medicine, athletes not only want to get well from their injury, they want to be better than they were before their injury,' so that puts a lot of pressure on the doctor to not only get them over their injury but to make them faster or better. This [being a surgeon] is a spiritual thing. Coaching, running, or track and field, I think there is a spiritual element to everything. If doctors don't have that spiritual element they really miss a lot. We're given these runners, and if we can help them a little bit then that's all our job is."

As always, David would face a bad situation and take a positive approach to this potential career ending injury. To this day, he is still grateful to Dr. Baxter for the second chance he was given, "'It was the best of times it was the worst of times.' I cannot thank him enough for giving me the opportunity to pursue my athletic dreams. I still smile and laugh to myself, when he told me 'I asked you to show me your face before I went under anesthesia.'"

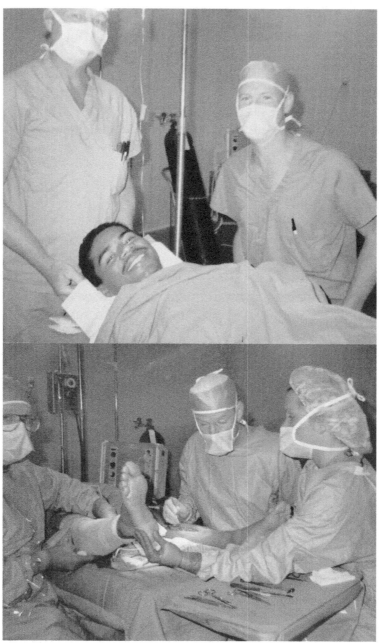

Dr. Baxter performs the surgery to relieve David's compartment syndrome on both shins.

Chapter 12
'85 Season: A return to great times

When an athlete has a lost season due to surgery there are always several questions following their return. First and foremost, is the question of how successful was the surgery? There is the question of longevity; how long can I stay competitive? For many sponsored athletes, there is the question of what impact will my injury have on my sponsorship? The athlete has that lingering question in the back of their mind, "Will I be good again?"

For David, his return to action following his 1984 season proved to be quite impressive. In 1983, he had broken the 1:45 barrier four times; in 1985 he would do so five times. In 1983, David lowered his PR to 1:44.39; in 1985 he lowered it to 1:43.35. Unlike 1983 though, where David had six first place finishes, his 1985 season would result in far fewer victories. In 1983 he was the top American half miler, but as the build-up to the 1984 LA Olympic Games and the subsequent seasons following, half milers in the USA and the world reached new heights.

An example of this can be seen with David's SMTC teammate, Johnny Gray.

During their days in CIF L.A. City competition, David dominated his rival from Crenshaw High School. Gray acknowledged in a 1996 *Chicago Tribune* article by Philip Hersch why he was beaten so regularly by David in the early part of their careers, and how him being his teammate made him so much better, "They [David and Crenshaw HS teammate, Jeff West] loved the sport when I only liked it," Gray said. "Being around them again [at SMTC] excited me to give it another shot."

Gray's career would go on beyond the 90s, and in addition to being the American record holder for the 800 meters, he has also broken 1:45 a mind boggling twenty-six times during his career. He became an Olympic finalist in four straight Olympics (84-88-92-96) and took home the bronze in the 92 Games at the age of 32. When Gray retired in 2001 his competitive career (HS, college, and professional) had spanned an inspiring thirty-five years. His 800 meter American Record set in August of 1985 still stands, and of all the events in track and field contested in the Olympics, is the longest held American record.

David's 1985 summer season began in earnest at the TAC Championships in Indianapolis, where he placed fourth running 1:44.77

behind Johnny Gray (1st in 1:44.01), John Marshall (2nd in 1:44.53) and Earl Jones (3rd in 1:44.58). Once in Europe he continued his successful return to competition from injury.

Over a period of eight days in August he would break the 1:45 barrier four more times. On August 21st in Zurich, David ran 1:44.57 finishing sixth behind Steve Cram, Joaquim Cruz, Johnny Gray, Sammy Koskei, and Rob Druppers. Two days later in West Berlin, he would run 1:44.39 equaling his lifetime PR finishing fourth behind Cruz, Gray, and Koskei. Two more days later he ran 1:44.49 in Koln finishing seventh behind Cruz, Sebastian Coe, Gray, Druppers, Agberto Guimares, and Koskei. Three days after that on August 28th, he would set his still standing lifetime PR of 1:43.35 in Koblenz finishing third behind Cruz and Gray, who would set the American Record of 1:42.60. Despite just being one year after his compartment syndrome surgery, David displayed the amazing finishing speed that he had relied on throughout his entire career. His final 200 meters at Koblenz was the fastest of anyone in the field. David was back.

Despite being a U of O Duck as a freshman during David's last year as a Duck, Claudette Groenendaal got to know David while traveling in Europe for the summer of 1985 season. "I knew of David when I was a freshman in Eugene, but I doubt he knew me. The men's and women's track programs (under coaches Bill Dellinger and Tom Heinonen) were very separate."

Even though 1982 was the first year of a combined men's and women's NCAA championship meet, Claudette recalls that the Ducks' men's and women's teams did not travel together or stay in the same lodging. Women's track and field had changed from being the AIAW to the NCAA and Claudette recalls, "Some of the men's coaches at that first combined championship meet were quite vocal about how adding the women would ruin the men's meet."

It was during the break between the two halves of the summer season in the town of Bern, Switzerland that she and her training group of Joaquim Cruz, Agberto Guimares, Jose Luis Barbosa, and their coach Luiz de Oliveira trained with David and the Santa Monica Track Club group with Joe Douglas. This was her introduction to Coach Joe Douglas, the Santa Monica Track Club, and David Mack. This bond of training and friendship would extend well beyond their competitive careers.

David sets what would be his lifetime PR of 1:43.35 in the same race that
friend and teammate, Johnny Gray, would set the American Record of 1:42.60.

Chapter 13
American Record in the 4x800 Relay in '86

Following his successful compartment syndrome surgery in July of 1984, David turned in an absolutely amazing follow-up season. Not only did he return to action, but he had made considerable improvements on his phenomenal 1983 season. David found "reasons to succeed."

The 1986 season would not be an Olympic or World Championship year, but Coach Douglas knew that his top two half milers had just run an American Record and the third fastest American performance of all-time. Perhaps the Santa Monica Track Club team could garner a World Record. The WR in the 4x800 meter relay belonged to the 1982 Great Britain team of Peter Elliott (1:48.8), Gary Crook (1:46.2), Steve Cram (1:44.6), and Sebastian Coe (1:43.9) who had crushed the previous record held by the USSR by over six seconds. Douglas thought he had the makings of a team that could challenge the Brits' mark. An SMTC team of Mack, Gray, West, and Earl Jones had run 7:12.96 in April of 1985 at the Mt. SAC Relays, and Douglas knew they could go even faster.

They would give it another shot at the Mt. SAC Relays a year later. According to the Mt. SAC Relays archives, "When the Santa Monica Track Club's Johnny Gray, David Mack and Earl Jones ranked Nos. 1, 2 and 4 in the U.S. last year, relay fans started looking for a fourth member. He turned up in veteran James Robinson.

"With no real competition available, each runner was a solo act. But they still managed to clock 7:06.5, less than three seconds off Great Britain's 1982 WR time of 7:03.89.

"Robinson got off to a slowish start (1:49.8), but the record chase was on when Mack followed with 1:46.7. Jones went all out, opening his 1:45.2 carry with a 49.9 lap. Gray started more conservatively, barely (50.2), and closed the race with a 1:44.8.

"Urged by his runners, Coach Joe Douglas immediately started seeking another crack at the WR. 'They can run under 7:00,' he opined. 'What's more Gray, Mack and Jones all could run under 1:42 this year.'"

Whereas the British team had run their mark in the middle of summer and had been pushed for three of the four legs by the British "B" team, the SMTC performance was all the more impressive as it was contested in the cool conditions of April with essentially no one nearby to push them. Their time broke the old American record mark of 7:08.96, set by Arizona State in 1984 [and the converted 4x880y mark of 7:08.0 by the 1973 Chicago TC team]. Their AR would hold up until August of 2006 when another SMTC team (Jebreh Harris, Khadevis Robinson, Sam Burley, and David Krummenacker) would run 7:02.82. David ponders on what his 1986 team might have been able to run if they, like the current AR team, had competition [the 2006 AR team finished less than half a second behind the winning WR team from Kenya] and raced later in the summer.

Mack splits a 1:46.7 for his leg, and hands off to Earl Jones.

Chapter 14
World Championships in '87

With David having such a good rebound following his 1984 surgery, he knew that the 1987 World Championships in Rome would validate the hard work he had put in following the loss of his bid for the 1984 Olympic team. A successful World Championship meet would also send a powerful message to Nike, who had dropped their sponsorship of David, but was picked up by Mizuno. Unfortunately, all the hard work he had put in to reach his goals for the '87 World Championships and '88 Olympics in Seoul, would lead to David developing an iron deficiency. He would supplement his training with iron injections given to him by SMTC team doctor, Dr. Gary Nitti.

David qualified for his second World Championship team by finishing third behind Johnny Gray (1:45.15) and Stanley Redwine (1:45.47) running 1:45.49 at the TAC Championship meet in San Jose on June 27th.

David ran his fastest 800 meters of the season in 1:45.03 at the site of his 1983 and 1985 PRs at a tune-up race in Koblenz on August 13th finishing fifth behind Billy Konchella (1:43.98), Abdi Bile (1:44.60), Faouzi Lahbi (1:44.72), and Harald Schmid (1:44.83).

At the World Championships more than two weeks later, David ran a tactical race in the opening round of the qualifying heats. He guaranteed his advancing to the next round with his fourth place finish in heat five of six heats. His time of 1:49.47 would be the slowest time of the thirty-two qualifiers heading into the quarter finals the next day.

In the quarter finals, fellow Americans Redwine and Gray would not advance, but David was the final qualifier for the semis with his 1:45.68 in the second heat. Of the two semi finals races the first heat would be the faster of the two heats, which meant that the two fastest non-automatic qualifiers (top 3 placers) would come out of that heat. David's sixth place finish in heat two and his time of 1:48.49 would not be enough to make the finals.

As a 26 year old professional runner with a family to care for, and less sponsorship and appearance money going to him as the 17th ranked 800 meter runner in the world, David decided that the 1988 season would be his last, and that he would start looking for other employment options. David would conclude his running career as the second fastest all-time US 800 meter runner. In the thirty years since the conclusion of his running career [as of

77

September 2018], David sits 7th on the US all-time 800 meter performer list: 1) Johnny Gray 1:42.60; 2) Duane Solomon 1:42.82; 3) Clayton Murphy 1:42.93; 4) Nick Symmonds 1:42.95; 5) Mark Everett 1:43.20; 6) Boris Berian 1:43.34; 7) David Mack 1:43.35. Coach Joe Douglas reflects, "If he hadn't gotten injured in 1984 and gotten sick, I think he could've been the world record holder [1:41.73 by Sebastian Coe in 1981 at the time of David's retirement].

David looks back on his decision to retire, "Just to know that I had a successful surgery with Dr. Baxter, and I was able to come back. After surgery there are so many unknown variables that you just don't know about. I didn't feel like I had that gear anymore; I used to just launch [in the final 110 meters]. To not have that anymore was like watching a doppelganger of your former self out there. You're haunted by it as you come off that final curve with a 110 to go and you know that you could just shift this thing into overdrive and blow these people away like you used to do at Hayward Field. But you just fear that this gear's not there; my body was different."

In a somewhat wistful reflection, David acknowledges, "Even though I ran my fastest ever [PR 1:43.35 after the surgery], it's just different. When I ran my fastest time and set my PR, Johnny and I both theoretically broke the American Record, but I had the fastest closing 200 meters in that race [Koblenz 1985]. So that tells me too that it was the combination of not having the confidence that I used to have. How could you have the fastest 200 meters if you don't have that gear? So, I had it [the final gear following his surgery], but with all that I was battling with the iron deficiency [1987 season] it was just so frustrating."

David getting after it in a 10km road race with his SMTC teammates. His range of 45.3 (400m) to 52:29 (15km) is phenomenal.

Chapter 15
LAPD Years (1988-1997)

With his career as a professional track athlete done, David sought out other forms of employment. As a former wannabe gang member, looking to become a police officer might have been seen as one of the least likely options for a career choice. For David though, it made good sense. He had seen how his neighborhood had been decimated by crime, gangs, and drugs. What better way to help fix the problems than by being part of the solution.

He reflects on his upbringing and exposure to the police in his neighborhood, "As a youth growing up in Compton, I was a witness to and a victim of police abuse. I was hanging out in the school parking lot across the street from my house, and the police came over asking us what we were doing there at 1:00 in the morning. We were just hanging out, but they punched us in the stomach, told us to get our asses home, and that was it."

David had a unique introduction to a potential career in law enforcement when he was in high school, "In my criminal justice class during my senior year of high school, it came at a point of my life when I had just begun reading, so I was reading everything I could get my hands on. My instructor was dating this cop from LAPD. He looked at me and said, 'I know that kid over there.' I looked up and said, 'Okay, what did I do?' 'You should think about being a cop. I've seen you run, and you're pretty good.' My teacher knew that her boyfriend used to play for the [Washington] Redskins. And she knew that I was a Redskins fan. Well now he's got my attention because I didn't like him until I heard that. And he thinks I should be a cop? And there it is. And that's how the seed was planted."

We often never realize the significance of the connections we make in life, but David had a connection to joining the LAPD through a former teammate. According to Locke High School teammate and LAPD veteran officer, Leonard Miller, "After high school, I went into the military and we stayed in touch throughout his college years. After I had come on the police department and he was done with his professional running career I talked to him about joining the LAPD, and he was like 'Man, I've thought about being a cop.' But he had some issues with the police, so I had to coach him to get him through the interview process. He had to overcome two things: One was a grand theft person and the other was an evading police officers. I helped him know how to answer their questions. Once he got hired we worked together off and on for eight to nine years until his incident."

Even with a new job, David did not forget his teammates and friends at Santa Monica Track Club. In fact he would rely on Coach Douglas and SMTC training partners to get ready for the challenges of police fitness. Claudette Groenendaal remembers, "I think it was during his training for the Police and Fire World Games in 1989, but he wasn't fit. I had to run a Time Trial effort over 600m, and he came to the workout that day. He was heavy. He took his shirt off, and he had this spare tire. He had been lifting but not running. He did the workout with me, and he did the Time Trial with me and even though it was January or February, it was like 1:29, and that off of zero training on his part. Then we came back, and I had to do a couple of 400s, and David ran around 55-56. Here he is: this out of shape, overweight guy running this on sheer grit because he was so competitive. It amazed me how he was able to dig deep and pull that out of there; it must've hurt like hell. He's really tough." David and his LAPD 4x400 and 4x100 relay teams would capture gold medals at those World Police and Fire Games in Vancouver, B.C. with impressive 3:22.59 and 43.41 times.

David began his career with the LAPD as a patrol officer. He spent many of his shifts patrolling the same neighborhoods he had grown up in. He hoped that he had become part of the solution. On some occasions, he would stop by the homes of the elderly parents of his friends and teammates from elementary school, junior high, and high school. On one patrol, he dropped in on former Locke High School teammate Gary Kelly's parents' house. Gary told David how much that had meant to her and to him. David was touched, "I had no idea of the influence that I had on his life. You don't realize that the things that you do when they're genuine how impactful they are. Gary told me, 'I knew you were special because when I came home, Mom has a picture of you on her wall. You are the only one who is not a family member on the wall. My Mom would say, 'Just guess who came by to see me?' Gary's parents were empty nesters by then, and I would go by in the neighborhood when I was on patrol for LAPD and check in on them."

During David's time with the department, the LAPD had become rife with an ever dissolving difference between right and wrong. The March 3rd, 1991 arrest and beating of suspect Rodney King by LAPD officers Stacey Koon, Laurence Powell, Timothy Wind, Theodore Briseno, and Rolando

Solano would focus America's attention on one of the first video recordings of police brutality. Then Los Angeles mayor, Tom Bradley, would create the Christopher Commission, which would investigate the structure, operation of the LAPD, and its use of force following the Rodney King beating. The report acknowledged, "Police work is dangerous. A routine arrest may suddenly turn into a violent confrontation sometimes triggered by drugs, alcohol, or mental illness. Neighborhood gangs often directly challenge an officer's authority. To cope, police officers are given the unique right to use force, even deadly force against others." Two of the findings of the 1991 report found that "a significant number of LAPD officers repeatedly used excessive force in ignoring department guidelines" and "the failure to control these officers is a management issue at the heart of the problem." Los Angeles Chief of Police Daryl Gates would resign upon the recommendation of the report's findings.

The officers' subsequent acquittal in April of 1992 resulted in six days of rioting in which 63 people were killed and 2,373 more were injured. Ferment and unrest permeated Southern California. With the LAPD and local police forces unable to regain control as looting, vandalism, violence, and fires spread, causing over $1 billion in damages, Governor Pete Wilson deplored the National Guard, and President George H.W. Bush sent in the 7th Infantry Division and the 1st Marine Division.

David looks back on the riots as "a combination of events." He reflects, "It wasn't just the verdict but the totality of things going on at that time: the whole political climate, the Latasha Harlins' killing, the judge [Karlin] giving the lady [her killer, Soon Ja Du] probation; the phrase could've come out back then, "Black Lives Matter" and it appeared that nothing mattered. You see it with your own eyes, and it created a separation within the department. You would be sitting with guys, who were white officers that you thought were cool, spent time with, or hung out together with, but when it came to that [the racial tension at the time] they could not see that it was wrong. It shattered a lot of relationships and the illusion that we were all Blue Officers, and we were not."

Ken Scott, fellow LAPD officer, Police Academy instructor, and 1989 World Police and Fire Games teammate offers his perspective, "I think that's reflective of society as a whole; not just a police problem. It goes across all walks of society; we're not over our racial divisions yet."

The 1991 Christopher Commission Report became a paradox for David as he saw this issue of the use of force versus stated department policy firsthand. His training in the Academy ran completely contrary with the real world experience of what he encountered on the streets. "When you get out of the Academy and get in the black and white [patrol car] with your training officer, the first thing your training officer tells you is to forget everything you just learned in the Academy. 'All that shit they taught you – forget about it because it will get you killed.'"

"My first day on the job, I could've been fired. The person who recruited me, Leonard Miller [former Locke High School teammate and friend], told me 'Look, you're going to see some things you don't like, but you're a probationer, so just shut your mouth and go along with it. My first radio call, I'll never forget it. It was a 415 [disturbance], male, unknown trouble, possibly under the influence of narcotics, so here we go. We arrive and this guy is in the car arguing with his wife, and they've got a two or three year old in the car with them in the front seat. We asked him to step out of the car, but he doesn't. They're sitting there arguing and the baby crawls over to the father, and he takes the baby and slams it against the door panel of the car where the mom was. He strikes the mother a couple of times, and that was it. I give my training officer credit, because I knew a lot of officers that would have waited for back-up to arrive, but he was like, 'Fuck that,' and he ran to the driver's door just as the guy was getting out. He was a lot bigger than my training officer, and they began struggling. He grabbed my training officer by the neck and was choking him. I came up from behind him, put him in a choke hold, and laid him down. He pissed on himself, knocked out. The choke hold they had taught us in the Academy is outlawed, and you can't use it anymore. So why the fuck did they teach me that."

"You know what my training officer said? He said, 'Good job. You will never have a problem while on probation from here on out.' It's because they want to know how you're going to react in a crisis situation. Over 50% of the officers freeze up. They [those that would've frozen up] would've drawn their guns and yelled, 'Stop! Stop!' which doesn't help me when I'm getting the shit beat out of me as their partner. They expect you to get in there and help, and I did. My training officer wrote in the follow-up report, 'The suspect was going for my partner's gun, and he had a situation where he could have shot him or choked him out.' I choked him out, but I could have used deadly force. That was my indoctrination; welcome to LAPD."

David realized that department regulations helped create a culture where some officers became scared to intervene. "You get into situations where an officer puts out a help call, and you get there and the officer is in the street fighting with somebody that's 5150 [involuntary psychiatric hold] or somebody under the influence. There were just two officers and this person. I was just riding along with this guy, and he just drove around the corner. I said, 'What the fuck are you doing?' He says, 'Oh, we were in the line of fire.' I was like, 'Dude, they were fighting; there weren't even any guns drawn.' I was like, 'I can never work with this guy again.' because he was too scared to get involved."

"There a lot of people like that, and they really shouldn't be in law enforcement. Those are the people who are going to kill someone because they can't go up there and physically deal with the situation. I had a situation where I was working a graveyard shift, where they had this 20-something, white guy who was in a stolen vehicle and had been in a police pursuit. He finally crashed, and they had him trapped. You've got twelve officers there, and they've got their guns pointed at him. He's like, 'F*** you, I'm not doing nothing.' They're yelling at him to get on the ground, and he's not being compliant. These guys can't think for themselves because all they can do is what they were taught in the Academy. I told them, 'Listen, I'm going to take him down, so don't shoot me in the back.' I was pissed off when I got there. All these officers, and you guys can't control this situation? So I just walked up there, and he was still yelling. I smacked him across the face, threw him on the ground, and handcuffed him. That's all you do; take his ass down. You don't need to stand there like he's Superman. That was it. When I put him on the ground, there was no more getting up."

Not all of the arrests that David was involved with became a demonstration of force. He remembers that his treatment of a suspect was largely dependent on the manner in which the suspect behaved and responded to the officers' direction. "People in the streets do a lot of dumb things. You dictate the treatment that you will be given. If you are compliant, I was going to treat you like a decent person, but if you were a threat to me I'm not just going to shoot you like they're doing now-a-days. I'm going to break you down. I guess having grown up on the streets, fighting and things like that, that didn't frighten me."

David remembers a story that could have gone much differently had he not had the presence of mind to read the situation and convey to the suspect that other options were possible. "There was this guy, who had just gotten out of the penitentiary; he was like 250 pounds. He was yoked up; big from lifting weights for the last fifteen years of his life. He had come home, and his wife was seeing another guy now. He was mad and wasn't going to leave her place. I got there as the secondary unit as a back-up. I assess the situation, and I see that they've got two young daughters, and they're crying because their dad is threatening their mom. She wants him out, and he's not leaving. He's black, and I'm the only black officer there, so I took the lead on talking to him. I said, '[His name], I don't think I can whoop you by myself. In fact, I don't think that two of us can take you. But you've got to understand, there's six thousand officers in the city right now. So even if you were to win this one, even if you were to kill two of us, you would die here tonight. This doesn't make any sense. You're going to lose either way; whether you get arrested or if you're going to die, but the only thing your daughters are going to remember is the police killed their daddy. So whatever is going through your head-- how angry you are, you've got to put that aside and think about your girls. This is what I'm willing to do: Right now, it's not so much a crime. I can take you wherever you need to go to diffuse this situation, and I know you have a lot of pride, so if you're willing to do this for your girls, I won't even put handcuffs on you.'"

"He said, 'I don't believe that.'

"I told the other officers, 'Hey, I got this,' and they know me. They all went out. I told him, 'You've got my word. It's just you and me. You've got the advantage right now. So you can walk out that door on your own accord in front of your girls with no handcuffs, and when we get in the car, I will take you anywhere you want to go.' He couldn't believe it. Because a lot of times, you've got to know how to talk to people to diffuse situations. You can't just be, 'Well, I'm in charge, and I'm telling you what to do.' You've got to try to reason with them. It was just the opposite of the story about the twelve officers trying to get the car thief to comply. He refused to get down on the ground, and he wasn't posing a physical threat to them. So I went in and took him down. Whereas, this guy wasn't going to comply and he was a physical

85

threat. The only way to bring him down was to kill him. I looked at it like, 'Is this really the legacy that you want to leave for your daughters just to see their dad die at the hands of the police? Is this really what it's about for you?' And he understood. He complied. He went downstairs, got in the car, and I took him to his mom's house. The wrong officers. The wrong situation. They get in there fighting with him. A gun goes off with those little girls in there, and they get hit or killed... you've got to be able to think."

The LAPD found itself in another maelstrom in June of 1994 as it responded to the brutal murder of Ron Goldman and Nicole Brown Simpson in Brentwood. The trial of accused killer OJ Simpson would cost the City of Los Angeles nearly $10 million and provide another focusing of the country's attention on the work of the LAPD. While David had been a part of the West LA division that was part of where the murder had occurred, he remembers the 60 mile low-speed pursuit of OJ Simpson and the white Ford Bronco driven by his friend, Al Cowlings, "I was so uninterested in that. I had been in enough high speed pursuits, to see that was like watching grass grow."

David offers his assessment of his time with the department, "You come in and you're 'green', full of enthusiasm, thinking you're going to make a difference in society especially when you grew up in the inner city, where you've experienced a few bad policemen. You don't want to be that cop; you want to be a better person — a better cop to the community. But eventually you become jaded, and you recognize that the problems in society are much bigger than law enforcement. I like to use the adage 'People are not born criminals'. Circumstances in society criminalize you; they make you who you are. Take the current immigration situation: people are fleeing from their countries because the United States and our allies have made their countries so intolerable that they're fleeing just to live. And you're saying that if you cross this imaginary line, 'You're a criminal'. So you either stay there and die, or you risk incarceration. The issues in society and law enforcement, particularly in a big city like Los Angeles are way beyond this so called 'enforcing the law'. I wasn't one to just follow orders blindly. I wasn't going to do it. I came in as an already grown adult, who had been around the world and had grown up in poverty. I had a different way of doing things, and I saw things from a different perspective."

David remembers an incident where the janitors were protesting in downtown L.A., and the police were sent in to stop the protest. David asked himself about this enforcement, "Why? Why are we using police resources against people who are non-violent and simply engaging in peaceful protest? It went against all of my ideologies because I believed that they did have the right to assemble and protest. Why should I stop them or be used as a resource to stop them? Most people are like sheep, and they believe what they hear. They can't really think for themselves because we as a society have been dumbed down, just trained to follow orders, and not to think. I didn't have many colleagues that were independent thinkers. It doesn't make me right, but these were my philosophies, and this is how I chose to enforce the law."

David provides an example of his philosophy in action. "A lot of people got breaks that could've gone to jail. Now, I don't condone drunk driving obviously [because his son was killed by a drunk driver], but if I pulled you over for drunk driving I would give the person two choices depending how inebriated they were: 1) they could give me their keys, take a taxi home, and then pick up their keys the next day when they were sober; or 2) go through the whole process of DUI, car to impound, and go to trial. One hundred percent of the time, the people said, 'Thank you, officer.' I'd have them turn off the engine, take their keys, and wait for a taxi to come pick them up. If you were an asshole, and arguing, then it was, 'Step out of the vehicle!' and you were gone. Your attitude always dictated how you were going to be treated by me."

David offers his view on the current economic situation, "If you look at the problems that people are going through, it's often mostly economical. 'Poor people make poor choices.' There was a large homeless population in the Rampart area. I was on a bicycle for a foot beat unit of the parks, and we would come in and give them a few minutes to gather their stuff and move along. Then the trash trucks would come in and gather all the remaining stuff left behind [by the homeless]. Now we have this gentrification movement going on in downtown L.A.. The people who have the means are moving in, converting the low income housing into lofts and upscale apartments, and the rents are going up. This has forced the poorer people out. They're pushed out of downtown and out into residential communities. So now you see many more homeless people out on the streets that weren't there before. They were pushed here. This is not a problem of people being vagrants; this is a problem of people having nowhere to go. Provide for them. And even if they are on drugs, that's no reason to say, 'We are going to cast them into the abyss.' No, they still have a right to exist, to live. That doesn't mean that you have to be flushed down the toilet or pushed to the limit where you have to commit crimes just to survive. The problems are so big; you can't help but become jaded."

David saw even bigger problems happening in society when he began working undercover. One of the things that David knew with his promotion to Undercover Narcotics Division was that his job became infinitely more dangerous. On one occasion in October of 1993, his job was to drive his partner into an area where they had planned to buy from a known dealer. David was not at his best as he was suffering from a migraine, but his supervisor wanted David in on the buy because he knew that David knew the area, and, even at less than 100%, would be better than anyone else they had. David explains, "Basically he [his supervisor] didn't trust the people that we had, because often people in law enforcement are cowards, who get their courage from their badge and their gun. It is what it is. But he knew that I was cut from a different cloth. He told me, 'I just want you to support [David's partner]. If something goes sideways, I know you will handle it.'"

When David and his partner drove up, the suspect was already on the sidewalk, and he walked up to the car with a gun in his hand. Instead of coming to the passenger side he proceeded to David's open window. His partner gave the seller the money, and told him he wanted to get a "twenty" [of crack]. He took the money but grew suspicious. David tells how the deal went sideways in a matter of seconds, "He [the seller] said, 'I've been beefin' with [one of the local gangs]; are you sure you're not [gang] bangers?' 'No, we ain't bangers; we're smokers.'"

David tried to convince him by showing him their crack pipe and other drug paraphernalia to lend credence to their story. The money they had given him was marked so that when the back-up unit came in to arrest him, they had more evidence for their case. Mack and his partner had already alerted their back-up but they were still out of sight and just a few minutes away. David continues the story, "He says, 'I don't know; I've never seen you guys before.' This was nothing unusual because dope dealers were just trying to protect their little enterprise. So this was not something we'd never encountered before. Then he puts his gun to my head. I already knew, and had been trained, that when in a gunfight never to run but to shorten the distance between you and your assailant. One, that shocks them; and two, there's a good chance they're not going to hit you. Then you will be closer to them, so that you can shoot them. When he had his gun to my temple, I just turned my head away from him because I knew he was going to shoot me. I had accepted that. I was armed and had my hand on my gun, but he couldn't see it. It's [David's gun] a semi-automatic, so that means the slide is going to go back, and there's a high probability that it's going to get caught on my shirt because it's underneath. I'm only going to get one shot off. One shot? I might just as well shoot myself in my arm. So as I turned my head, I slowly brought my gun out, and he goes to grab it from me. I shot him two times, and he didn't get a round off. It knocked him back three feet, and I shot him again. Each time it would knock him back, so I opened my door and unloaded on him. And then he finally went down. The reason it took so long for him to go down was that he was on PCP.

"There was another guy with him with his hand under his shirt. He was so lucky that I had tunnel vision [on the seller], and I had assumed my partner was dealing with the second guy. Unfortunately, as all this was going down my partner had gotten behind the tire well [of their undercover car]. That's when you find out how people respond in critical situations. He basically just hid out, and I dealt with it. And the only reason that thirteen old kid didn't get killed that night is because I had run out of bullets. When you work undercover, you don't carry extra magazines. Meanwhile all the black and whites are zoomin' in; unmarked cars are coming in at ninety miles an hour, screechin', ready to lay out anything that's moving. Even though my gun was empty at this point, I ordered him to get on the ground, and he complied. That was it."

"I was on the job six years before I took a sick day. The job took the best of me, and I just didn't care anymore. It was a decent salary once you added overtime. Having done the job, I'm not bitter about it. I just don't look at the police as heroes; you're a paid civil servant not a damn hero. Over 50% of the cops that I've seen were cowards. They weren't putting their life on the line. They weren't entering buildings if they were in danger. They were waiting for backup units so that the odds were in their favor."

Even after earning an LAPD Medal of Heroism, and rising to the ranks of Senior Lead Officer, David saw that his enthusiasm was gone. This police force had become mired in controversy and scandal, and, at the same time, David sunk to the lowest point in his life. Arrested December 16th, 1997,

David was lodged in Montebello City Jail and eventually the Metropolitan Detention Center in downtown Los Angeles for a federal crime. There is so much already written about David's fall that anyone who is interested can certainly look up its details. In researching the crime he committed, it is important to recognize the manner in which the media foisted judgment on David, vilified his character without ever getting the whole story, and often wrote things that were patently untrue. Lost amidst the sensationalized stories and the scapegoating the LAPD posited for David's arrest is the reality that a young man, who had been an exceptional and highly regarded police officer, a husband, father, teammate, and friend had now made a decision that would impact all of that.

Subsequently, many people possess opinions about David without knowing the whole story. Nigerian novelist, Chimamanda Ngozi Adichie, speaks to this notion of falling into the trap of "the single story" in a 2009 TED Talk, "All of these stories make me who I am. But to insist on only these negative stories is to flatten my experience and to overlook the many stories that formed me. The single story creates stereotypes, and the problem with stereotypes is not that they are untrue, but they are incomplete. They make one story become the only story."

The bottom line is that David acknowledges his responsibility for what had landed him in federal prison with a sentence of fourteen years and three months. David could have very easily allowed this circumstance of his life to destroy him. Instead, he responded with the maxim that has guided his life: "In life you have to find and focus on the reasons to succeed and not the excuses to fail."

Ed Williams, Ken Scott, David, and Leonard Miller of the LAPD win gold in the 4x400 (3:22.59) at the 1989 Police and Fire World Games in Vancouver, Canada.

Chapter 16
Prison Years: "Graduate School"
"The ultimate measure of a man is not where he stands in moments of convenience or comfort, but where he stands at moments of challenge and controversy." — MLK

His life, no longer the life of a champion athlete or that of a civil servant, instead had become inmate #12866-112 in the federal prison system. His fall became even more bleak since now he would be living in prison as an ex-law enforcement officer. David decided it would be best to keep a low profile and try to stay fit and study.

Following his sentencing, David was sent the 1,874 miles from the Metropolitan Detention Center in downtown Los Angeles to a low security facility named the Federal Correctional Institution at Waseca, Minnesota, which is 75 miles from Minneapolis. Taken into receiving and distribution, he was placed in "Administrative Detention" (aka solitary confinement) during the in-take in order to be sorted out. David soon realized that his time in prison was not going to be made any easier by the administration. "The warden came and told me [being ex-law enforcement] that I wasn't welcome in this institution. It wasn't like I had signed up for a vacation here; this is where I was sent. He told me, 'I'm going to do everything in my power to put you where I think you should be.'"

The warden proceeded to arbitrarily change David's security listing from low (first time offender) to medium/high so that he could transfer him out to a higher security prison. After about two months of "Administrative Detention," David was moved another 216 miles to a medium security penitentiary in Oxford, Wisconsin, where he would undergo more time in "Administrative Detention" until he was sorted. "They had painted this whole false jacket on me that I was a gang member; a 'shot caller' or a leader." At the first administrative meeting with the warden and the SIS (Special Investigative Services), they told David that some of their informants had indicated that "they were affiliated with his [David's] gang" and that if he tried to clique up with them they will know through prison informants. "I told them that I was not a part of any gang, and that I was sorry that they believed what had been written about me [in the media], but I'm not a gang member."

Things at Oxford went well at first as David became acclimated to prison life; keeping fit and working in the library. Things became far more difficult and potentially deadly as national news announced that he was a primary suspect in the murder of rapper, Christopher Wallace (aka Notorious B.I.G. or Biggie Smalls). As a result of this news, during the middle of the night, David returned to "Administrative Detention" or "Protective Custody". David scoffs at the administration's use of euphemisms, "It's the same thing whether they call it "Administrative Detention," "Protective Custody," or "Solitary Confinement". Call it what you want; you're still in the hole."

After another two to three months in Wisconsin, David was re-designated again and taken the 384 miles from the Federal Correctional Institution (FCI) in Oxford, Wisconsin to Southern Illinois FCI at Greenville, which is east of St. Louis, Missouri, and south of Springfield, Illinois. David gained insights into his move to Illinois, "There's a saying, of course I didn't know what it meant at the time, but I would soon learn: 'You can't get any further South than Southern Illinois.'"

Having been ex-law enforcement meant that he was always at risk. With the addition of these media sensationalized allegations of his involvement in the Christopher Wallace murder, David's life would become even more precarious. One such incident occurred in December of 2000 while in the exercise yard of FCI Greenville. "I was working out one evening, and the gym is divided into two structures with a passageway about twelve feet long and eight feet wide connecting the two. It was about ten to fifteen degrees out so it was cold. I had been lifting weights and working out real hard, and I decided to go weigh myself. I went down the passageway to weigh myself, and I was coming back, but the light was out. There were six people in the passageway planning to kill me."

Using "rocks in socks" the six assailants hit him on the back of the head trying to knock him out. One of the six, armed with a "sharp object" stabbed David repeatedly and punctured one of his lungs. "I felt this 'boomp, boomp, boomp' on my back, so I turned around and started fighting. I thought I was fighting two people because by it being dark I couldn't see how many there were. But they couldn't see me either, and so by fighting back that turned things into chaos. I hit them as much as I could. Then I ran back into the rec room where the scale was because I knew there were pool sticks in there, and I wanted to grab a weapon."

David's instincts probably saved his life. "After I had gotten the pool stick, and they had walked in, they were trying to walk normal, but now I could see that it was six guys. I just started splitting wigs with the pool stick. It turned into a big donnybrook until the guards hit the alarm and came in to break things up."

Had the six assailants succeeded in knocking him out, they surely would have killed him.

David had been stabbed seven times, one which punctured his lung, and he received two lacerations on the head. If one of the stab wounds to his back had been a fraction of an inch over, it would have lacerated his spinal cord leaving him dead or paralyzed.

Having been ex-law enforcement, the guards had held David with an air of contempt and had viewed his desire to "walk the yard" [inhabit the general population instead of spending his time in "Protective Custody"] as an affront to their authority. David recalls an administrator apologizing to him saying, "I'm going to tell you something, but if you ever tell anybody I told you, I will deny it. There are people here that have taken it as their mission to make sure that you get hurt or killed."

During the course of the follow-up investigation by the SIS on his attack, they revealed to David that they had received earlier death threats on his life before his attack. According to David, "They thought these were bogus because no one had ever acted upon them [the threats]. What that told me was 'You were aware of it, and you didn't do anything.' Having had the background in law enforcement and knowing how to read and write, I took that little grain of truth that they had inadvertently revealed to me and wrote and filed a motion to sue the Bureau of Prisons. In his motion, David alleged that "[defendant SI Greenville, et al] acted with deliberate indifference for the plaintiff's [David] safety in failing to protect plaintiff from a known and foreseeable serious threat to plaintiff's safety and life, by consciously disregarding the excessive threat to plaintiff's safety in subjecting plaintiff to the threat of death."

David became a jailhouse lawyer with the help of a book recommended by the Southern Poverty Law Center that taught him the ins and outs of filing a motion, writing a bivens, or preparing a writ. He credits this group as instrumental in his legal efforts while in prison. As a display of his gratitude, he still donates to their organization to this day. From Greenville,

Illinois he would partake in another 415 miles of "Diesel Therapy" landing him in FCI Manchester, Kentucky. The experience of almost being killed in prison would lead David to an emotional crossroads. He reflects on this stage of his life, "I began embracing the prison culture. This was a real fork in the road for me, where I almost went the wrong way, but I was pretty fortunate."

David planned to enact a vendetta and send a message in his new location by stabbing one of the gang members associated with the gang that had made the attempt on his life in Greenville. A man who worked in the ceramics shop made David a ceramic "bone crusher", which would go undetected by the metal detectors throughout the prison. Knowing who their gang's shot caller was, David plotted his revenge. "I was on a revenge trip, and I wanted to let these mother fuckers know that this wasn't going to be a one way street. I was going to come up to him in the rec yard and stab him as many times as possible, but the thing of it was that I would have probably killed him like a shark in a frenzy. So I took the 'bone crusher' and hid it in one of the empty lockers in our unit. But that morning, SIS came in and got me after only being there for two weeks. They cuffed me, took me back to the hole, and they told me that members in Manchester of the gang that had attempted to kill me in Greenville had tried to get another gang to join them to get me. That additional gang didn't want to have anything to do with them, so they went to SIS and told them what was going to go down. SIS told me that since I was the problem, they were taking me off the yard. I'm basically looking like I'm organizing all this, but I wasn't; I just wanted to hit one person. They made me the shot caller, but there's this phrase, 'In the land of the blind, the one eyed man in king.' So there I am. I liken it to Leonard Zelig in the Woody Allen movie. You just assimilate to the environment. I had unfortunately started to assimilate. I had almost been killed, and I wanted some revenge."

Once again, as David traveled down this shadowy path, he would be met by another angelic presence to help direct him another way. David met his case manager, Mr. Hallman, who would give him another perspective on this recent turn of mind. "He pulled me into his office, and he told me, 'Mr. Mack, I'm old school. You're here as punishment; you're not here to be punished. A lot of my colleagues want to punish you because you're ex-law enforcement, but I'm not like that. There's a lot of things going on, and I can't help you until you help yourself.'"

This time David would be transferred another 386 miles to a maximum security United States Penitentiary in Lee, Virginia. The USP at Lee recognized that David didn't belong there, and that his presence would only incite others to act. As David was being processed during his arrival, getting ready to go out on the yard, there was a lockdown due to a stabbing of some members of the same gang that had tried to kill David by another gang on the yard. Had David been on the yard at the time of the stabbing, he most certainly would have been caught up in the violence. "That was another learning opportunity," Mack reflects.

His next stop would take him another 122 miles to USP Lewisburg in Pennsylvania, where a sign at the prisoners' entrance quote the words of Dante's *Inferno* "Abandon all hope, ye who enter here." As all of this was going on in each of the prisons that David was being shuffled to and from, the news media continued its field day of coverage of the murder of a prolific rap star portraying it along with the murder of another rapper as a West Coast vs. East Coast revenge murder. As David's name continued to be dragged deeper into the mud, the next move for David would take him even farther and farther towards the east coast. David surmises, "They were really orchestrating my demise." The SIS at Lewisburg indicated that while David was there, he would never be allowed on the yard as a safety precaution for himself and their guards.

As he continued to wait for his day in court with the BOP, David, was transferred 838 miles further south. He found himself in FCI Talladega, Alabama, which is a medium security prison one hundred miles from Atlanta, Georgia. David liked the change of security, and he looked forward to the opportunity to be back in the yard again. The BOP saw things differently though, "Unbeknownst to me, they have a whole unit that's designated for long term housing segregation that you never get out of. That's where the Cubans were held [121 Cuban inmates from the Mariel boatlift housed there for over a decade before rioting in August of 1991]. That's where they'd designated me. I'm not laying down; I'm fighting because I'm headed to court."

While David had begun his legal work for his suit against the BOP in Manchester, Kentucky his time in solitary confinement provided him with time and motivation to prepare for his case. "I'm in my 6x8 foot cell by myself, which is good because I've got my routine. I exercised every day because I had to rely on my physical prowess to protect myself. I meditated. I read. And I studied law. When I meditated, I took inspiration from Mahatma Gandhi, who told his supporters when he would fast to protest, 'The mind is its own place.' It could make heaven out of hell or hell out of heaven. So he wasn't suffering. When I meditated, I pictured myself still on the European circuit. I went all the way around the world. I escaped all the time. You can not house my brain; my spirit. I'm running up and down San Vincente Blvd. I'm on the beach. I'm gone! I escaped many times, and they never knew it. Then I'd come back. I've got my books. I'm reading Howard Zinn [*A People's History*], real histories, and biographies. I read *Hurricane: The Miraculous Journey of Rubin Carter* [wrongfully convicted middleweight boxer who eventually was exonerated]; *The Last Man Standing* (David Baldacci) a biography about Geronimo Pratt [a decorated military veteran and a high-ranking member of the Black Panther Party, who was falsely accused and served twenty-seven years in prison before being freed]; *The Long Walk* by Sławomir Rawicz; Nelson Mandela's [*The Long Walk to Freedom*]. To see what I was going through was nothing compared to what they went through. I was like, 'Dude, you got no excuse. Get your shit together.' It helped me to focus, and having my legal work gave me incentives. 'Tomorrow! Something big is coming.'"

Finally, after exhausting all of his administrative remedies, which David described as "a hurdle that you are made to go through to try to get you to say, 'Fuck it' and get you to quit." Instead it only made him more determined. "At one point during the initial proceedings, I had a moment of validation. You have the circuit judge, and under the circuit judge you have a magistrate judge. The magistrate judge had ruled against me in one of my motions against the BOP. Now I have ten days to refile, and here I am working from the hole trying to get as many of the law books that I could get my hands on, and find the cases that were applicable to my case. I'm a lawyer; a jailhouse-fucking lawyer. I don't have a computer either; I'm handwriting all these motions in ink, and they have to be legible. Not only legible, but it has to have bearing on my case. It has to have case law with proper citations. So I go to the circuit judge and explain to him that the magistrate judge had ruled in error and had misinterpreted the law on my filing. When that magistrate judge ruled against his circuit court judge on my behalf, it was over. I had graduated law school; I'm a lawyer now. The world opened up. You can't stop me now."

David had his day in court back in Illinois (540 miles away). "When the judge ruled on my behalf, they did a writ to bring me back to Illinois to go before the judge for my suit. They have to assign me a lawyer because I had been working 'pro se' [representing himself]. The attorney that the court had assigned me in Southern Illinois was this young, white girl with her paralegal with her. She had probably just passed the bar and was just learning. So she came in there to meet me for the first time, and I had definitely fallen into the prison culture, so I am sure her first impression of me was not too favorable. I looked the look. So my assigned attorney that's supposed to be helping me takes the first hour and a half of our attorney client visit telling me why I didn't have the grounds to sue them [the BOP] that I thought I had. So we're going back and forth and round and round. So finally, I knew how to diffuse her [having been ex-law enforcement]. I said, 'Let's just stop. We're clashing, and I know you want to help me. I know you do. That's why you're here. So help me to understand what you're basing your opinion on that I don't have standing for a suit, and here is the law that I'm citing.' She showed me where she was making her point from, and I told her, 'You are absolutely right, and I agree with you, but look at subsection exception blah blah blah.' When I read that to her, her face turned red. Oh, I had embarrassed her in front of her paralegal by showing her case law and how to apply it."

"The next day in court, she instructed the judge that I had called her and told her that I did not want her on my case, and said that I couldn't work with her. She just lied to the judge because I had embarrassed her. I was in shock. The judge asked me if this was true, and I said, 'Your honor, no sir. I could go into detail, but I tried to work with this lady, and I think she may have been a little bit embarrassed or intimidated, but I need representation.' The judge said, 'Mr. Mack, I've read your briefs and you're very articulate. I've heard you speak right now, and even though you're entitled to an attorney, I think you can probably tell me your story better than any attorney. Would you like to [represent yourself]?'

"I went up there and told him everything the BOP had done, and how other BOP officials had told me that they were trying to kill me. From my first reception where I was told [by the warden] that he was going to bump me from a low security to a high security prisoner to the USP. The attempts on

98

my life. How they knew of the threats and didn't act upon it. When I got done the judge looked down at the BOP attorney and said, 'Let me ask you a question. Don't you have Martha Stewart in custody [found guilty in 2004 of felony charges of conspiracy, obstruction, and making false statements to federal investigators, and was sentenced in July 2004 to serve a five-month term in a federal correctional facility]?'

The BOP lawyer replied, 'Why yes, your honor. She's in federal custody.'

'Well, you don't have her in a regular facility do you?'

'Oh, no your honor. She's high profile. We could never do that.'

'Well, let me tell you something. Mr. Mack, here, is more high profile than Martha Stewart. Not only is he ex-law enforcement, but he is alleged to be involved in the murder of a very high profile rapper, and there's a war going on out there between the east coast and the west coast. Do you want me to re-designate Mr. Mack where I think he should be?'

'Oh, no your honor. We were just in the process of doing just that this morning, and we have re-assigned him to FCI Butner [North Carolina].'

"Now mind you, I had filed this suit and had gotten it all the way to here. I didn't know anything about FCI Butner, but it is on the east coast in the deep south, so I told the judge, 'Your honor, I'm not sure if I feel safe there.'

He told me, 'Well, I think this a good facility for you and if you have any trouble there, you have my number, and you can call my clerk, and I will re-designate you.'"

With the judge eventually ruling in his favor and re-designating him as a high profile prisoner, whose life was in potential danger, and who would be better protected in a low security prison, the defendants in the case, the BOP, responded to the judges ruling by sending him the final 798 miles of his diesel therapy to FCI Butner in North Carolina. FCI Butner would become famous in 2009 when former chairman of NASDAQ, Bernie Madoff, would receive a 150 year sentence there for stealing over $20 billion from investors in the largest Ponzi scheme in US history.

After over four and a half years of his five years served while being in solitary confinement, FCI Butner was an entirely new experience. "I went there and went through R & D. I'm so used to waiting for the unit team and getting placed in "Administrative Detention" until I was processed. None of that. I got my bedroll. Got my unit and cell number assigned. It was like a campus. I'm looking at grass. I'm looking at trees. Where the hell am I? We're still surrounded by concertina wire, but I was able to relax, and you don't have to be so hard anymore."

With his final transfer, the personable Mack had little trouble finding "friends". In prison, things were segregated by racial groups. One such group that Mack befriended might have been an unlikely association. "These guys were Mafia. There was a guy named Carmine Persico, and he was a big Mafia boss. There was a guy named Jersey Joe, and he was known as having the most hits. He was my handball partner. The dudes never argued with us. It was just a persona we had. I was one of the few people of color that they would invite to eat with them because everything was segregated inside. Carmine invited me to their table. And you're judged by the people you associate with. So I'm sitting at the Italian table eating food with them.

"There was this little, tiny guy; a world class speed skater. He was an Italian guy named 'Muscles'. He was called that because he was so small and had no muscles. We were in a Physics class together. He was always in the way. I was like 'Dude, can you move to the side? Why are you always up at the board?'

"He replied, 'Because I can't see.' I tried to hold in my laughter, but I told him, 'I'm sorry.' So we ended up becoming friends, and because it was physics, he began to give me a little help. He asked me, 'I always see you running and working out. I've always wanted to do something like that.'

"I told him that he should do something, being a little white guy in prison you don't want to get victimized. So I told him, 'I tell you what. I'll give you a program', and he started running with me and lifting weights. He was so excited getting in shape; he'd tell me that he had run a 10k, and he was so proud of what he had done."

"We took a class together — Employment Law. We were the only two people taking this online class. We would do our work and take the tests, and then we would cross reference each of our answers. If our answers were different, we would debate and ask, 'Why?' We sharpened each other and made each other better. Then the instructor came and asked to talk to the two of us around the mid-term. He said, 'You guys are embarrassing me. You guys are doing better on your own, on this online course than the class I'm teaching in person. I don't know what you're doing, but continue to do it. I tell my class about you guys.'"

"Then in an English class, 'Muscles' wrote a paper about us called 'Opposites Attract'. He was just this little scrawny guy, white, Republican. I'm black. I was like 205-210 pounds, so I appear to be this big black guy. A democrat. We became friends."

His notoriety as a former LAPD officer turned felon led to a great deal of media backlash. With his reputation as a rogue cop planted in the public eye, it might have come as no surprise when stories began to surface about David's involvement in the 1997 murder of a famous rapper. This case has remained unsolved to this day, but David's name became connected to the murder because of a paid informant's testimony linking Mack and his LAPD partner to the killing. The LAPD and FBI were under pressure to solve the high profile case, and Wallace's family brought a $500 million wrongful death civil case against the LAPD, David, and his partner. So in the midst of dealing with his own incarceration, David now had to serve as his own lawyer to disprove the allegations of the civil case.

According to David, "When they were saying that I was instrumental in the murder of this prolific rapper, I was facing murder charges. I was representing myself; 'pro se' or no attorney. I wasn't an ordinary prisoner: 1) I was literate; 2) I could read the reports; 3) I had nothing but time; and 4) I was innocent. So when I was doing my legal work [preparing his defense] I was out of solitary confinement and placed in the general population. People found out what I was doing, and they would ask me to help them with their [appeals] cases. I would tell them, 'I don't want your money; you don't have to pay me.' I told them, 'I can't because I am my most important client. I am not going to devote the time to your case as I am to mine.'"

"I was able to go through what looked like a criminal investigation, but turned into a civil suit. Basically, I blew that whole thing out of the water because it was all false."

His experience facing potential murder allegations gives him the chance to pause and reflect now more than a dozen years later, "You see so many people now freed after 30 or 40 years in prison, and it's just so sad. I see what they tried to do to me firsthand. And these people [the wrongfully incarcerated] don't know how to read police reports. They don't know how to show that all this shit is manufactured."

"After I had gone through all that and was writing my own rebuttals and briefs, the city [of Los Angeles] tried to distance themselves from me and they wouldn't give me an attorney. I wrote a brief and the judge brought me down [from prison to L.A.] on a writ that I had written. I requested to come down and defend myself, and the City Attorney tried to say, 'Hey we want to join forces with you.' But I was like, 'No, you blew that opportunity. I am representing myself, and you are an adversary to me as much as they are.' That's when the city went and got me an attorney. And when they got me an attorney, it happened. They did what they should've done to begin with. When my attorney went and talked with the family's attorney, they said, 'This is what we want to do. We want to offer your client [David] money that will make the money from his crime that he was convicted of look like chump change, and all we want him to do is take the fifth.'"

For David that didn't sit well with him. He chose to take the higher ground, "You know, morality counts. I had an opportunity to make millions, but I turned it down because of the principle. You've dragged my name through the dirt. You've vilified my character. You made me look like the next biggest criminal since Scarface, but I said, 'No, you can take your money and stick it up your ass.' All I had to do was take the fifth, and the inference would be that I was hiding something. And they were going to pay me for that. My attorney said, 'I can't tell you what to do, but whatever you do I have to assist you. And that's that. He was shocked that I wouldn't take the money."

"It was the same thing when the FBI came to interview me while I was in prison and asked me if I wanted a deal. I said, 'I don't want a deal. I'm going to do my time [for the crime he was convicted of] and you can stick your deal up your ass.' They said, 'Well, we'll bring charges on you when you are about to get out.' I said, 'Good, I'll see you at the door. Until then, goodbye. That was it.'"

"At the end of the day: 1) I'm a moral person; 2) I'm a stand-up guy; and 3) Whatever I did, I'll take my medicine. I'm not going to drag other people down. It is what it is, and that's life."

In part due to David's efforts, the FBI and LAPD dismissed Mack as a suspect in the murder. The family's case was dropped as the earlier testimony began to unravel. In a June of 2005 *L.A. Times* article by Chuck Phillips, "The informant, questioned under oath in a civil lawsuit, also admitted that his identification of the alleged gunman was fraudulent. He described himself as a paranoid schizophrenic. He said he had no solid information that ... Mack was involved -- only 'hearsay.' And he acknowledged that he had never laid eyes on [the third person he'd earlier identified as the shooter] when LAPD detectives showed him six photos and asked him to identify the suspect."

One of the things that David is most proud of during his time in prison is the impact that he had on others. He was able to convince two fellow inmates to get their GEDs (Graduate Equivalency Degrees). "I told them, 'You're not always going to be in prison. You've got to start thinking about what you're going to do when you get out.'"

Another person that David impacted came from a very unlikely source. After getting out David received a letter from an inmate who was a Neo-Nazi, "Before I met you, I didn't like blacks. I didn't respect them. All they do is come in here and watch television and play games. I've learned to respect you. I didn't like you when you first came because you were ex-law enforcement, but you stayed to yourself; always in your books. Always disciplined."

This quality of David's permeates many that he encounters. Whether it be a neighbor, teammate, a competitor, or fellow inmate, David's impact on others is far flung. While awaiting sentencing to prison, many former neighbors, teammates, and friends rallied to support him. His neighbors wrote letters to the judge on his behalf extolling what a pillar of the community he had been in their neighborhood.

One of the first people that David met at the University of Oregon, was Matt Westman, a basketball player who came to Eugene from Eastern Washington the summer of 1979. David and Matt lived in the Sigma Chi fraternity house that Art Boileau had helped secure for David when he arrived that summer. Matt recalls being taken by David's intangible presence or spirit that he exuded even as a college freshman, "I remember being so impressed by David during that first year. You could just see that he had 'It'. While it is hard to define exactly what 'It' is, you could definitely see it from David."

Matt's friendship with David continued until Mack left Eugene. Matt recalls reading all the stories in the news about David's professional running career and his retirement from running, and his joining the LAPD. He heard from Eugene friends about David's arrest and read with disbelief of the many stories in the news.

Matt, a Christian, was praying one night asking God for a sign of what he was supposed to be doing with his life after a move to the Bay area in 2002. "It seemed strange to me then, but I was told by God to pray for six different people, and one of them was David Mack. Each night I would pray for him even though I was never fully sure why."

Sixteen years later, Matt and David would reconnect, and Matt shared the story of his experience with Mack. David, moved by Matt's story, told him that this was during the time that he had been in solitary confinement during his sentence. Sometimes we never see or understand the work of the Weaver when we look at the tapestry of our lives.

Former Stanford Cross Country and 10,000 meters All-American and former SMTC teammate, Ellen (Lyons) Santiago tells about her desire to assist David as he underwent the process of studying solar energy. The books that she sent him to study were "returned to sender" because they had been sent to the prison from a private individual and not directly from Amazon or the publisher. Not to be deterred, Ellen reached out to the publisher, and they were able to send the necessary books plus some additional ones. Ellen's persistence she said was because David needed to know that there were people who still loved and supported him. Yet again the fabric of our stories often overlap. She had known David since her time as a Stanford runner while David competed for the Oregon Ducks. After college their careers became reunited as teammates running for Joe Douglas with the Santa Monica Track Club. She remembers one occurrence when she was heading out of her apartment for a morning run. She had brought the kitchen trash bag out to deposit it in the curbside garbage can. On the way down the stairs of the apartment complex that several SMTC athletes also lived in, she stumbled down the stairs causing quite a commotion in the early morning hours. She recalls that it was David who hurried to her assistance to make sure that she was all right. Ellen recalls, "That's the kind of person David is. He was always looking out for the people around him. Making sure that he could get those books that he needed was the least that I could do for him."

Another former teammate, U of O sprinter, Jeff Norris, also reached out to support David during his time in prison. Jeff knew what David was going through because he too had spent time in federal prison. Both grew up just a few miles apart, ran in the same L.A. City section, ran for U of O as teammates, and shared the common experience of doing time while their wives raised the family during their time away. According to Jeff, "It's been a very unique bond, and we've remained friends through it all. I came home from prison before David did, so I filled in the gap for his son. His son and daughter respected me because I knew them from birth. Whatever his wife needed when David was away, I was there. I would tell her that the progress I've made with my life since coming home will be the same, if not better, for David when he comes home. It will be because of his work ethic. He has always been a very determined person to fulfill good things, and he's always helped everybody and anybody."

David looks back on all that he experienced during his thirteen plus years in the federal prison system, and he offers this reflection, "I discovered a better part of me in the BOP."

David still has his prison ID to serve as a reminder of his time that helped him to become the better person that he is today.

**David takes great pride in knowing that he inspired
two fellow inmates to get their GEDs.**

David received his AS degree following his time in prison.

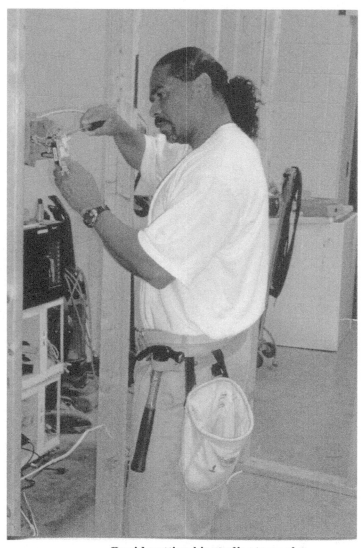

David putting his studies to work.

Chapter 17
A Redeemed Life

Released from prison on May 10th, 2010, David at 48 years old, sought to use the skills he had studied while in prison and move forward with life. His two children were no longer children anymore, and David looked to be that father they deserved but had missed out on.

Finding employment as an ex-felon is often a big hurdle for those recently released from prison. Using the knowledge gained while in "graduate school" and the same tenacity he demonstrated as a champion runner, David found work as a solar installer and now works as a project manager for a company that installs electric charging stations for electric vehicles. Don Ward, former Duck teammate observes, "The thing that I find so impressive about David is that he was incarcerated for thirteen years, and upon his release, he's been without employment for a total of one and a half to two weeks."

David loves working in renewable energy. "I've never been more satisfied with what I'm doing. It's so rewarding; so much more challenging. You're using your brain and not just your brawn. I just have to pinch myself because I had the foresight, but I didn't envision it blowing up the way it is because I was in solar initially [now in EV charging stations]. When I was in "graduate school", I had the foresight that solar and renewable energy was going to be the next big wave; I needed to prepare myself for that, and I did. I like to use the analogy that I'm standing in the middle of the desert with my surfboard or inflatable raft in hand, and I'm ready to ride the tsunami of renewable energy. When I was teaching, I would always tell my students that renewable energy — specifically solar — is an industry that if you just put your raft in the water you will stay afloat; meaning that you will always have employment. But if you put your raft and your oars in the water, you can go as far as you want to. I'm a perfect example of that. I put my oars in the water, and here I am: a project manager for one of the biggest companies in the United States for EV infrastructure."

When David got out of prison he earned his Associate of Science degree from Trade Tech College in renewable energy (solar, wind, and thermal energy) taking classes after work in the evenings. David's education in graduate school and following gave him time to develop his attitude about the fate of our world; it is the result of much reading and a strong belief in humanity. He holds out hope for us and our planet. "The world is moving on, and the writing is on the wall. It's unfortunate that the people are not seeing this. They're hoping that the world is going to be beholding to the oil companies and the coal industry. No, technology is moving forward; we're at the crossroads now like when the automobile replaced the horse and buggy. Mother Earth can't take it anymore; we're destroying the climate and ourselves. They're are a lot of progressive countries that are trying to change things. The world is changing, and I just feel so fortunate to be right here in renewable energy."

One of the first encounters David had to reach out to someone and share his experience of being in prison came about from a class on solar energy that he was asked to teach by a former teammate from the Santa Monica Track Club. David sat in on the class and was discouraged with the lack of curriculum the instructor taught from, "He [David's SMTC teammate] had a guy who knew something about electricity, but he was just reading verbatim from the book. After sitting in this class for thirty minutes, I told my friend, 'You don't have a curriculum. You just have a guy reading out of a book. You don't even have a syllabus. If you want me to teach this program, this is what I'll do, and this is what I'll do it for.' He thanked me, and I created a whole curriculum, syllabus, and everything for him."

In class David had a student who had done time in prison, and during every break he would be complaining about the lack of jobs for ex-convicts. David got tired of hearing it and gave the student some advice, "I don't like that negative, defeatist, victim attitude. So I pulled him aside during break, and I told him, 'How much time did you do?' And he told me, 'Six years.' So I asked him how long he's been out, and he told me, 'Three years.' So I brought out my ID from my incarceration and showed him. I told him, 'I've done twice the amount of time that you did; I did thirteen years, and I've been out way less time than you. And I'm teaching you. What's the problem here?' And he said, 'I'm going to shut my mouth, and you ain't ever going to hear another word from me again.'"

David brings that same attitude with his experience when he speaks to the at-risk youth at the Compton YouthBuild program, which delivers workforce, leadership and educational opportunities for under resourced and economically disadvantaged young people from Compton, South Los

Angeles, and surrounding communities. According to David, "Poor kids whether you're from the ghetto, the barrio, or the trailer park, if you can't identify with them — if you can't let them know that, 'Hey, I've been where they've been' — then they're not really interested because even if you've got a good heart and good intentions, but you don't know what it's like. When I told those kids [from the Compton YouthBuild] that I was from Compton, and that I grew up having to eat out of trash cans, and how poor I was — I had them. These kids know bullshit when they hear it. I told them, 'No matter what you do in life, never forget that you're special, and you might not hear it from another person, another friend, another family member, and you may not believe it yourself, but you need to know what I'm telling you. You can do anything you want to accomplish. It's hard work because if it was easy, everybody would be doing it. It resonated with them, and they connected with that message.'"

One obstacle that David found upon his release was the naysayers. He took solace from those who stood by him and continued to see the good in him, "People that know me don't judge me by that one incident in my life, they judge me by the totality of my life. So I don't worry about those things in my life because those people that do judge me on those things are not my true friends to begin with. They are just looking for a reason for me to fall and denounce me."

Friend and Duck teammate, Jeff Norris, puts it in a philosophical light, "When everyone counted us out for being ex-felons, or the way that society portrays us, they say, 'You've been this way, so how can you change and become so successful?' Well, life isn't over. That's just part of the journey. We've just looked at it [their time in prison] as extended schooling. You learn so much by being away. You come to appreciate the time you have left. You become far more effective and far more efficient with your time."

While prison helped make David a changed man, many of the same qualities that had endeared him to so many friends, teammates, and coaches were all the more present. Claudette Groenendaal recalls one such incident, "I got a text about six years ago from David saying, 'Call me ASAP'. I called him, and he told me that Ellen [Lyons-Santiago] had breast cancer. When he found out, he and his wife drove up to the San Jose area the next day to take Ellen out for dinner. He had your back."

111

Just as his team during his time at Locke High School, University of Oregon, and Santa Monica Track Club filled that surrogate role of family when he was younger, Claudette Groenendaal sees the role that SMTC has had, not just on David, but on so many others, "The thing about the Santa Monica Track Club is that we're family. My teammates are like my brothers and sisters. When we get together, it is so great because I feel like we are instantly transported thirty years back in time because everyone jokes a lot and it's a nice camaraderie. Santa Monica Track Club is family. I'll never forget how they welcomed me into their group, and how everyone sticks up for each other is what makes SMTC so unique."

Upon his release, David became a welcomed member of the SMTC family again and still re-connects with Coach Douglas and his teammates. David acknowledges the role that Joe has had on him, "Joe is a father figure to me. We talk once a week. He is my life coach!" Coach Douglas fondly recalls the role that he has played in David's life, "I still feel like a father to him. He had such a rough home life as a child. When he came to work with me, he did what I told him, and I was very strict. I'd always check on him to make sure he wasn't staying out too late at night so that he could be at his best."

David acknowledges that he did not always make it easy on Joe to keep him from partying, "Joe blames himself [for not keeping David out of mischief], but I've told him, 'Coach, you could not harness us. The thing that I did listen to him about was finances. That's why I always say that Coach was my life coach, friend, and father figure. He didn't just give me track workouts; he gave me wisdom and knowledge. He tried to give me life experiences and guide me. He had this kid who still had these rough edges from Compton, but it was a transformation, although it was a slow process. Joe would take me to museums to expose me to culture. He was always trying to develop me beyond track. He did his best, and I really appreciate him for that."

Coach Douglas, who is now in 80s, says that he has trouble remembering things. As he speaks about David and David's career, it is as if Joe has been transported back in time recollecting the races and times of a decade's worth of David's performances. Just as Joe has had a lasting impact on David, David's impact on Joe is palpable. David says, "I joke with him a lot. When he says that he has dementia, I tell him, 'But coach, you still remember me.'"

While he has not jumped back into the competitive running part of his involvement with SMTC, he has taken up cycling and has risen up through the ranks of masters cycling as a Category 3 racer. His introduction to cycling resulted from having fallen off the roof at a solar installation project he was working on. In breaking his pelvis and dislocating his hip he began riding a stationary bike as part of his physical therapy. Still the competitor, this led to him joining a local cycling club, the Bahati Cycling Club, which strives to build community and support youth programs through cycling.

One such opportunity to do good for others occurred a few years ago when David and his cycling club volunteered to be coaches for the Junior Blind Olympics. The Junior Blind Olympics, puts on several Olympic-style events adapted for the blind for young people ages 6 to 19. Athletes come from California, Utah, Arizona, Nevada and elsewhere to compete in such events as rowing, shot put, 100-yard dash, archery, rock wall climbing and the long jump. David's impact as a coach proved to be long lasting, "I was this young boy's coach, and I was taking him around describing to him what he was going to have to do. It was a whole day event that I was helping him for. At the end of the day, we said goodbye as he got on the bus to go home to Arizona. The next year I did it again. I see the kid and I remember him and called out his name. He heard my voice, and he called back, 'Coach David!' It made me tear up because this kid had remembered my voice. His mom told me, 'You are all he's been talking about. His coach, David.' One of my teammates on my cycling team told me after seeing how this had impacted me, 'You know what? A coach told me a long time ago that when you're dealing with kids it doesn't matter if you win or lose. When you look back on your life, you're not going to remember if you won a championship or how many games you won or lost. You're just going to remember that coach; if they were a good coach or an asshole.'" The unfortunate incident of falling two stories and almost being killed gave David an opportunity to grow, take up cycling, and do good for others in the process.

With all of David's near death experiences (1. Almost shot by his Godfather; 2. Hit by a car in 6th grade; 3. Attempt on his life by gang members during the summer of '76; 4. Gun to his head in 10th grade; 5. Nearly drowned freshman year in Willamette River; 6. Nearly drowned in Lausanne, Switzerland; 7. Gun to his head during an undercover buy; 8. Attempt on his life in prison; and 9. Fall from two-story building), he reflects on his life from a unique perspective, "As an atheist, I really have to question that there might be a higher being and a source and meaning for your existence whether you want to believe it or not."

It is true that David's life has been filled with many moments that would cause someone to stop and reflect. Perhaps it was his time in prison that gave him a new focus on life. Norris offers this perspective on David's worldview, "It's been a real blessing to have a friend like David. He says he's an atheist, but when you listen to him speak, he talks about 'How blessed...' and 'How fortunate...'. You can't be blessed by a higher being without acknowledging it. He acknowledges it in a subliminal way. He says he's an atheist, and he knows I'm a Christian, but never has he tried to impose his values on me. Or persuade me to believe the way he believes. He says, 'Jeff, you're a man of faith, and he knows that and respects that in every aspect. That just shows you a lot about who he is and his character. He doesn't make people feel that they have to believe and think the way he thinks. That is what I love about David. He has his voice, and he lets his voice be spoken. Despite how you feel about it, he is going to voice his true values and true feelings, but he's not going to say that you have to believe that way or walk that way, but I respect you for the way that you walk as long as it is 'right'. As long as you are upright in the way that you walk around me and with me, I'm fine with that."

Johnny Gray offers his opinion, "It's unreal to hear that Dave was experiencing those things, but I'm glad that Dave got through those things [difficult childhood, arrest, prison, and the death of his son]. God has a will that's going to be done no matter what we think and feel. He put a lot on Dave, but one thing is that He won't put more on you than you can handle. Whatever Dave went through, it made him see that there is a higher being. That was probably God's way of getting his attention. Dave's a good man, and he's a man that stands for something. He thinks for himself, and he has his own mind. We all are humans, and we make mistakes and that's why Jesus died on the cross for us because he knew that we were going to sin. He told me that he had gone to see Jeff's [West] mother [West was killed in an automobile crash in December of 2000] after he got out, and I was really touched by that. God has a weird way of taking us through life, and we all have our struggles. What he [David] has endured, I don't know of any man who has endured that much. He had a rough life to experience all that at such

114

a young age, and then at the latter part of his life. Now he is in another transition of his life. He is at the third stage of his life, but I think that he now knows and understands life, and he can enjoy it. He understands his purpose in life; I'm just glad to see that my buddy is all right and not dead, but has overcome all those obstacles."

David's world became shaken in November of 2011 when his twenty-five year old son, while riding his motorcycle home from work in downtown L.A. was killed by a drunk driver. By the same principle that guided his life during hard times, David made the decision to help raise his son's children as his own. Hearing him speak of his grandchildren with such love and devotion affirms the notion that perhaps the reason for David surviving all those near death experiences during his five plus decades on this planet comes down to something as simple as these words of 18th Century English writer Samuel Johnson: "There is a sacredness in tears. They are not the mark of weakness, but of power. They speak more eloquently than ten thousand tongues. They are the messengers of overwhelming grief, of deep contrition, and of unspeakable love."

David confronted this overwhelming grief in November of 2018 when he traveled to Egypt to memorialize his departed son on the seventh anniversary of his death. Thanksgiving is a particularly difficult holiday in David's household because his son's passing occurred just days leading up to the holiday that traditionally celebrates family. David, his wife and daughter placed their memorial to their son and brother in the "Valley of the Kings" or the "Gateway to the Afterlife" along the Nile River.

David explains, "We always try to do something to get away from home. It's a way for us not to deal with it so emotionally. We celebrate his birthday, and we remember him on his passing as well, but we celebrate his life. I had thought about it and had wanted to take my son's ashes and lay them to rest in the Nile there, but I wasn't ready. 'I can't do it.'" David saw that following the tradition of leaving a stone monument to memorialize their deceased loved one was fitting with them being in the "Gateway to the Afterlife".

"We set it up there and had a moment of silence and laughed because my son had such a sense of humor like his Dad and his sister. I talk to my son all the time; it's just something that I do. I always speak to him, and I laugh with him. I can hear his voice as if it were yesterday. I read somewhere that a person is never truly dead until the last person that knew them is gone. That is profound because as long as you have that memory they stay alive."

One of the things that I've observed in talking with David, his friends, teammates, and coaches is that as David has gone through life there seems to have been an almost angelic presence in his life. It is as if his biological mother was prophetic in naming him Angel. Looking at his childhood and the time when he was running for Coaches Yeoman and Strametz, Coach Dellinger, and Coach Douglas this presence of goodness has been palpable. It becomes a testament to the part of our lives that we just don't ever fully understand. We may not fully grasp it, but I think that we're on this planet for some reason, and we may never know it. In talking with these many people it has become very clear that not only have these people had an impact on David's life, but he has had an impact on ours. It is a powerful message.

Gray reiterates, "God bestows blessings upon us, but those blessings might not be for us. It is for us to share with others, and as we share those blessings bestowed upon us with others, those people share those blessings back upon us. I think that's just how the world goes. We help each other; we motivate each other; we protect each other as best we can."

David's life is a fascinating one. To consider where he came from; to see what he rose to; to envision the depths that he fell upon; and to appreciate the growth that he has experienced inspires us to reflect on our own existence. Through his tragedies, triumphs, trials, and transformation we get a new perspective into our own stories. Hopefully, by David's story, we see that we can choose to be beaten by life or we can choose to aspire to something greater.

Chimamanda Ngozi Adichie, in the same aforementioned TED Talk, provides a sense of perspective of the fabric of David's life stories, "Stories matter. Many stories matter. Stories have been used to dispossess and to malign, but stories can also be used to empower and humanize. Stories can break the humanity of people, but stories can also repair that dignity."

David, having lived many lives in his fifty-eight years on this planet, has woven a tapestry of stories quite extraordinary. It is a life that has touched the lives of many, and it is a life that has been influenced by many. It has been a life of struggle, success, shadow, and, ultimately, redemption. According to David, "It hasn't been a perfect life, but it's been a wonderful life."

David oversees a solar panel installation

David speaking to the youth at Compton YouthBuild

**1968 Mexico City Olympian, John Carlos, with David at a LA
Library Lecture Series event**

David in the fast lane pursuing his new sport

Former 800 meter rivals James Robinson and David
catching up on the good old days.

Former Ducks roommate and friend, Matt Westman

Two great Duck 800m runners: Wade Bell and David

**Olympic champion, Carl Lewis, Coach Joe Douglas, and David
at a SMTC reunion**

David with former Duck teammate Don Ward

A gathering of Ducks: Bart MacGillivray, Bill Dellinger, Jim Hill, and David

Epilogue:
David Mack On...

Training Hard:

"Joe [Coach Douglas] will tell you that he had a hard time slowing me down. It was never an issue to get me to work out; it was about slowing me down. I would be running down San Vincente, and he would be yelling at me to slow down. 'I can't,' I would yell back. It felt so good. He was always trying to harness me. I just loved to run and hammer. The same thing with [Coach] Strametz; it was always, 'Slow down!'

I remember [a teammate] when I was at the University of Oregon when we would do workouts in the graveyard across the street from Mac Court, oh my God, he'd complain. He'd be like, 'You got to slow down. You can't race like that.' I'd just look at him like, 'What's wrong with you?' I would just ignore him and start hammering him even more, and it would show in the race; he never beat me.

Because if you train hard, you're going to race like that. You can't train easy, and then when you get in the race expect to max out if you're not even used to being there. You don't know what that's like. Dig deep — from what? 'I've never been right here. I can't go beyond that pain threshold.'"

Toughest workouts:

"One I did with the late Jeff West in high school. During Christmas vacation, he and I trained together under his coach, Merle McGee. He gave us repeat halves (880 yards). I had to run them in 1:56, jog a quarter mile and then do another one. Jeff couldn't do it.

At U of O, I trained with a whole bunch of different groups; one workout I'd be with the half milers, sometimes the quarter milers, and then other workouts I'd be with the 5000 meter guys. We'd have repeat miles over at Amazon Park [barkdust trail]. Bill would send me to work out with Tom Byers of Athletics West doing repeat miles on Pre's Trails.

One of the workouts I remember [with Joe Douglas] in Helsinki when I didn't make the final [of the 1983 World Championships]. I was so primed and ready of course because it was obvious that after that I won most of my races. I beat Willi Wülbeck of West Germany, who was the world champion, in Berlin. Coach gave me a 500 meter workout. I don't remember the exact time [58.9 according to Joe Hendershott's *Track and Field News* article], and after I was done, he told me that I had just broken the world record. I was floating, literally, and I will never forget it,"

Coach/athlete relationship:

"Beyond that [having been coached by several great coaches] they were also good people who genuinely cared about me. Each coach I had, we bonded in a certain way. The relationship was beyond the surface of coach and athlete.That is rare because coaches have so many athletes, but we just had that special relationship."

Regrets in his training:

"One of the regrets that I have is dietary. Bill McChesney [U of O teammate] was the first person that I ever met that was so into the diet, and he would try to tell me, 'Dude, you've got to do this. You've got to do that.' I thought then that he was a health food nut. He had the right formula; he knew what he was talking about. He had done the research; his dad was a doctor. He understood biology and performance. I was just like, 'Man, why would I do that?' I was a junk food king; I ate garbage. So now I'm like, 'Wow, what if I'd put the right fuel in my body.' Another person I'd met that was very conscious of their diet was Mike Boit [Kenyan 1972 Olympic 800 meter bronze medalist]. I regret that I wasn't more serious and understood the importance of nutrition, and, of course, proper rest. Oh, my god, honestly, the night before I ran my PR, me and Johnny [Gray] were up until 3:00am partying."

Running after surgery and eventually calling it a career:

"I remember watching the Paralympics World Championships a few years ago [2017], and I became so fascinated because this one sprinter [Jarryd Wallace] who had won the 200 meters. He had to have one of legs amputated from the knee down due to a surgery that had gone bad. The announcer said he had compartment syndrome [just like David's injury] and tears just rolled out of my eyes. I had never been satisfied with my accomplishments because my goal had been to run 1:38, and I believed I could do it. Everything else was a failure. A lot of people will tell me, 'Man you ran 1:43!' But to me I believe I could have run much faster than that. I had never been satisfied with that [his PR] until I saw that guy, and it made me realize that at least I got the chance to pursue my dreams again [after surgery]. My 1:43.35 was the sixth fastest time in history, but it was only after seeing him run did I have closure.

With running, I used to get to a level where I felt like I couldn't slow down. It was such a great feeling to get there, but I never got there again. I never reached that level where I could just float and fly."

Delayed Gratification:

"When the time is right: it's going to happen, and it's just going to be that much better. I'm still advancing in my career, in my knowledge, and in my wisdom. So I believe all that if it reaches a pinnacle — or not — it's about the further or the longer it takes, the better it's going to be."

Literature:

"I love to read. I like humor, and there are just two books that I can recall that had me laughing, crying laughing that I read while I was in graduate school. One was *The Confederacy of Dunces* [by John Kennedy Toole]. Another book, Gore Vidal's *Lincoln,* had me cracking up; I love humor. I'm also a big fan of John Updike; the *Rabbit* series [*Rabbit, Run; Rabbit Redux; Rabbit is Rich; Rabbit at Rest*] are some of the best books I've ever read."

Staying Positive:

"I believe in that. I just had that conversation with a young guy that I work with. I could tell that he was bummed because we had met that big goal after a big push, and now we had to push again. I told him, 'Hang in there. You know what? Six months from now you're going to be, 'I can't believe where I'm at today.' That's because, you're going to be saying to yourself, 'I was tired, and you were pushing us so hard, but you know what, I believe it.'

He asked me, 'How do you stay so positive? Nothing gets you down. Nothing. We're all complaining.'

I told him, 'Because it's all temporary. You've got to keep it in perspective.'

He said, 'I wish I could get that.' So I divulged to him my background, and he was shocked; he could not believe it. He finally said, 'Now I get it; you've seen worse conditions.'

I told him, 'This is nothing.'"

Relaxing:

"I'm always listening to music; I keep one ear bud in. I listen to Chinese traditional music, Native American flute music… all soothing music. You've got to get out of that moment; all the stress. Walk away from your computer and take a walk, calm down, and relax. You know what? That big old mountain; I'm going to start knocking it down one scoop at a time. Stop looking at it as, 'How am I ever going to get up?' One step at a time. It helps to have that philosophy and that knowledge of understanding how to block out things, and the things you can't block out what to filter in and what to filter out. I'm not going to clog my brain with crazy, wild music that's going to have me amped up. I'm going to have therapeutic, easy listening music that doesn't result in noise pollution while I'm trying to think. I want something that keeps me calm, steady — not putting me to sleep — but it's therapeutic. It keeps me when I do get frustrated with something, it lets me go, 'Whoa. Easy.' It lets me figure it out, go on, and that's it. What I've also found out is that whenever you can't resolve or figure something out, if you sleep on it the answer is going to come because your brain is more intelligent than you realize. But your subconscious can't give you the answer because your conscious mind is so clogged with all the elements of the day: traffic, personal issues, relationships, the stress of work. When you let your mind calm, the answer comes right to you. No matter how big and insurmountable it seemed that day, the next day it seems so simple. 'Oh, my God. I was stressing over this.'"

His travels to Egypt (history):

"The trip was, on so many levels, amazing to me because I have studied African civilization, the destruction of African civilization. I read books by Dr. Chancellor Williams of Howard University [*The Destruction of Black Civilization*] and *Guns, Germs, and Steel: The Fates of Human Societies* by Jared Diamond of UCLA and so many other books that as you start to put this all together. So to actually have read beyond the average research on the African continent, in particular: the Nile, and the pyramids I find it interesting that it is not widely known that pyramids have been found in Sudan that precede those highly recognized one in Egypt. Civilizations are fascinating. They have been going on for eons, and there are civilizations that we will probably never discover during my lifetime. Just to know that those pyramids there have not even been really excavated, is just amazing. Then to go there and see it in person. To see the Sphinx, ride down the Nile, visit the different museums and see the culture of an ethnic group that we were derived from and to be here and to have been subjugated for so long and to be — for lack of a better word — brainwashed and just taught Black History from a 'slave perspective' existence rather than the original. Wow, what if people really knew where they actually came from and originated."

His travels to Egypt (civilizations):
"History is so long. I was visiting the Nubian museum and I was reading about these different [periods of] thousands of years that these people ruled this part of Egypt and then the Egyptians ruled and back and forth. I was like, 'Thousands of years?' That's just amazing to me. When you put it on the scale of your life span, and we see how old the United States is, you soon realize that empires come and go. And I honestly believe that we are watching the fall of our empire; it's imploding. It's just life. Nothing lasts forever; not the good times nor the bad times. Or empires. I love history and I'm always fascinated by it."

Extrovert or introvert?:
"I was an extrovert, but I have a small circle of really, really close friends. I talk to anybody, anywhere, but you just move on in life. I'm able to make friends and enjoy companionship wherever I go, but I don't feel like you have to nurture it monthly or yearly. I'm kind of like an oxymoron; I'm an extrovert, but I'm a loner as well."

Personal Spirituality:
"I think it comes from being open to and accepting the fact that you don't know everything. No one does. I've read so many different things about energy. Energy — you can't destroy energy, and we humans are energy. We

can change forms, and where does it go? We don't know. There are so many books — theological books — written about it [where we go], but no one truly knows. I accept that, and I accept people who believe what they believe. I don't try to convert anybody or defend my position. I have read, and I like to think that I am intelligent enough to base my decision on that."

Life and death:
        "No one really knows what transpires when we die. In my former career [as a police officer] I talked to people who are dying, and as we are having a conversation they actually pass away. I continued to talk to them and tell them, 'I don't know if you realize it or not, but you just died. I don't know where you're going, what you're feeling, what you're experiencing, if you're still conscious, and I wonder if you still hear me talking to you, but you have physically died.' I know that the energy is still in them because their eyes are still open, but I have to wonder, 'Where did they go?' Nothing changed other than the energy that energized their body is gone. We can't see it — the spirit — or whatever you want to call it; we can't see it leave the body, but I just watched a person die. It's amazing. It's not something you see everyday, aside from maybe people who work in hospitals. I just find life fascinating; every aspect of it."

Appendix

I. Seasonal 800 PRs

Year	Age	School/Club	800m	Major Meets
1977	16	Locke HS	1:56.7y	1) CIF LA City "B"
1978	17	Locke HS	1:51.8y	1) CA State
1979	18	Locke HS	1:50.2y	1) CA State
1980	19	U of O	1:46.67	6) NCAA; 6) OT
1981	20	U of O	1:46.03	5h) NCAA; 4) TAC
1982	21	U of O / SMTC	1:45.55	1) NCAA; 3) Bislett
1983	22	SMTC	1:44.39	2) TAC; 4sf) WC; 1)Koblenz
1984*	23	SMTC	1:49.21	7h) TAC; 8qf) OT

(*injured = compartment syndrome surgery)

Year	Age	School/Club	800m	Major Meets
1985	24	SMTC	1:43.35	4) TAC; 3) Koblenz
1986	25	SMTC	1:44.17	2) Koblenz
1987	26	SMTC	1:45.03	6sf) WC; 5) Koblenz

II. Other PRs

400m	47.15
400m relay split	44.5
600m	1:14.15
1000m	2:16.90
1200m relay split	2:58.2
1500m	3:44.85
1 mile	4:01.20
5k road	15:35
10k road	30:58
15k road	52:29

III. Career Race Results

Date	Meet	Event	Location	Place	Time
?/??/77	Locke vs. Banning	880y	Locke HS	1	2:00.4
5/21/77	LA City "B" Champs	880y	East LA CC	1	1:56.7
1/21/78	Sunkist Indoor	4x440	Los Angeles	?	3:26.4
3/18/78	League Dual Meet	Mile	?	?	4:26.5
?/??/78	Compton Invitational	880y	Compton CC	1	1:56.6

Date	Meet	Event	Location	Place	Time
4/08/78	Locke Invitational	Mile	Locke HS	1	4:31.7
		4x440		1	3:22.2
4/??/78	League Dual Meet	880y	?	?	1:56.1
4/29/78	Arcadia Invitational	800m	Arcadia	1	1:53.6
		4x440		2	3:18.7
5/05/78	Marine League finals	Mile	Carson	1	4:26.1
		4x440		2	3:20.5
5/13/78	LA City Prelims	Mile	Birmingham HS	1	4:33.2
		880y		2	2:04.4
		4x440		2	3:24.9
5/20/78	LA City Semis	Mile	East LA CC	4	4:29.9
		880		1	1:54.6
		4x440		2	3:20.3
5/27/78	LA City Championships	880y	East LA CC	3	1:55.5
6/02/78	CA State Championship	880y (sf)	Bakersfield	1	1:54.6
6/03/78	CA State Championship	880y (f)		1	1:51.83
1/06/79	Ali Indoor	1500m	Long Beach	1	3:50.8
1/20/79	Sunkist Indoor	1000m	Los Angeles	2	2:16.7
		4x440		3	3:29.7
2/02/79	Times Indoor Games	1000y	Inglewood	?	?:??.?
3/22/79	League Dual Meet	880y	?	?	1:55.9
3/24/79	Pasadena Relays	800m	Pasadena	1	1:52.74
		4x400		1	3:18.5
3/29/79	League Dual Meet	880y	?	?	1:53.5
		4x440	?	?	3:18.0
4/07/79	Eisenhower Relays	1500m	Rialto	?	?:??.?
		4x400		1	3:16.0(47.5)
4/14/79	Arcadia Invitational	800m	Arcadia	1	1:49.9
		4x400		1	3:13.1(47.1)
4/18/79	League Dual Meet	880y	?	?	1:50.6
		4x440	?	?	3:14.2
4/27/79	League Championships	440y (p)	Gardena	1	49.5
5/04/79	Marine League	440y (f)		1	48.9
		880y		1	1.55.5
		4x440		1	3.19.0
5/06/79	Pepsi Invitational	800m	Westwood	9	1:51.6
5/12/79	LA City Prelims	440y	Wilson HS	1	49.2
		880y		1	1:56.8
		4x440		1	3:18.0
5/18/79	LA City Semis	440y	East LA CC	1	48.13
		880y		1	1:54.9
5/26/79	LA City Championships	440y	East LA CC	1	48.29

		880y		1	1:50.7
		4x440		1	3:14.5 (47.7)
6/01/79	CA State Championships	880y (sf)	Sacramento	1	1:54.6
		4x440 (sf)		1	3:16.5
6/02/79	CA State Championships	880y (f)		1	1:50.2
		4x440 (f)		1	3:14.1
6/09/79	International Prep	880y	Naperville, IL	5	1:52.5
1/26/80	Portland Indoor	4x880	Portland	1	7:40.6 (1:51.7)
2/15/80	Sunkist Indoor	880y	Los Angeles	3	1:50.8
3/15/80	Oregon Invitational	DMR (1200m)	Eugene	1	9:51.31
		4x440		1	3 :19.0
3/21/80	Santa Barbara Invite	1500m	Santa Barbara	1	3:49.8
		4x440		1	3:14.5 (47.2)
3/29/80	UO vs. Tennessee dual	1500m	Eugene	1	3:48.8
		800m		1	1:50.57
4/12/80	UO vs. Kansas dual	1500m	Eugene	4	3:48.19
		4x440		2	3:12.16
4/05/80	UO vs WSU dual	800m	Eugene	1	1:48.2
		4x440		1	3:13.9
4/19/80	UO v. UW dual	400m	Seattle	2	48.1
		4x440		1	3:16.74
4/26/80	UO vs. BYU dual	800m	Eugene	2	1:47.81
		4x440		1	3:11.43
5/03/80	UO vs. OSU	800m	Eugene	1	1:48.75
		4x440		1	3:11.36
5/10/80	UO vs. Indiana dual	800m	Eugene	1	1:49.16
		4x440		2	3:11.0 (46.5)
5/17/80	Oregon Twilight	Mile	Eugene	3	4:04.29
5/23/80	Pac-10 Championships	800m (p)	Seattle	1	1:50.48
5/24/80	Pac-10 Championships	800m (f)		1	1:48.28
		4x440		4	3:10.79 (45.9)
6/05/80	NCAA Championships	800m(p)	Austin	1	1:47.55
6/06/80		800m (sf)		1	1:46.84
6/07/80		800m (f)		6	1:47.48
6/21/80	US Olympic Trials	800m (p)	Eugene	3	1:48.41
6/22/80		800m(sf)		1	1:47.02
6/23/80		800m (f)		6	1:46.67
1/30/81	Sunkist Indoor	880y	Los Angeles	5	1:54.5
3/21/81	Oregon Invitational	DMR(800m)	Eugene	1	9:40.69 (1:47.7)
		4x440		1	(46.6)
3/28/81	LSU Invitational	800m	Baton Rouge	1	1:47.18

135

Date	Meet	Event	Location	Place	Time
		4x400		1	3:10.14
4/04/81	UO vs. UW dual	1500m	Eugene	1	3:44.85
4/11/81	UO vs. Auburn dual	400m	Eugene	1	47.15
		4x440		1	3:13.9
4/18/81	U of O vs. WSU dual	4x400	Pullman	2	3:07.66
4/25/81	UO vs. Kansas dual	800m	Eugene	1	1:50.50
		4x440		2	3:17.6
5/02/81	UO vs. OSU dual	800m	Corvallis	1	1:51.94
		4x400		2	3:15.13
4/25/81	UO vs. Kansas dual	800m	Eugene	1	1:50.50
5/09/81	UO vs. Cal Berkeley dual	800m	Eugene	1	1:49.70
		4x440		1	3:11.45 (45.98)
5/16/81	Northern Division Relays	4x880	Eugene	1	7:31.36
5/22/81	Pac-10 Championships	800m (p)	Palo Alto	1	1:47.6
5/23/81	Pac-10 Championships	800m		1	1:46.99
		4x400m			DQ
5/28/81	Twilight Meet	Mile	Eugene	11	4:26.5
6/06/81	NCAA Championships	800m (sf)	Baton Rouge	5	1:47.62
6/20/81	TAC Championships	800m (sf)	Sacramento	1	1:46.34
6/21/81		800m(f)		4	1:46.03
8/11/81	Göteborg Invitational	800m	Sweden		1:47.98
8/13/81	Malmö Invitational	800m	Sweden	2	1:46.77
8/19/81	Zürich Weltklasse	800m	Switzerland	6	1:47.75
8/23/81	Nikaia Invitational	400m	France	7	47.85
8/28/81	Van Damme Memorial	800m	Belgium	?	?:??.?
1/30/82	Portland Indoor	1000y	Portland	8	2:13.7
2/05/82	Times Indoor	600y	Inglewood	4	1:11.1
3/20/82	Oregon Invitational	DMR(800m)	Eugene	1	(1:51.1)
		4x440		1	3:17.93
3/27/82	UCSB, Fresno, SOU 4-way	1500m	Santa Barbara	2	3:48.8
		4x440		1	3:11.9
4/03/82	UO vs. WSU dual	800m	Eugene	1	1:50.11
		4x440		1	3:17.93
4/10/82	UO vs. LSU dual	1500m	Eugene	1	3:45.11
		4x440		1	3:13.81
4/17/82	UO vs. UW dual	DNS	Seattle		(school)
4/24/82	U of O vs. Kansas dual	800m	Eugene	1	1:53.13
		4x440		1	3:14.99
5/01/82	UO vs. OSU dual	DNS	Eugene		(sick)
5/08/82	UO vs Cal Berkeley dual	800m	Berkeley	1	1:48.2
5/15/82	Oregon Twilight	Mile	Eugene	3	4:01.20

Date	Event	Distance	Location	Place	Time
5/22/82	Pac-10 Championships	800m	Eugene	1	1:48.11
		4x400		2	3:10.11
5/28/82	OSU Twilight	4x400	Corvallis	1	3:09.0 (46.7)
6/02/82	NCAA Championships	800m (p)	Provo	1	1:47.31
6/04/82		800m (f)		1	1:48.00
6/18/82	TAC Championships	800m (p)	Knoxville	3	1:48.05
6/19/82	TAC Championships	800m(sf)		DQ	1:48.06
7/07/82	Bislett Games	800m	Norway	3	1:45.55
7/13/82	Cork City Sports	800m	Ireland	1	1:46.48
7/27/82	World Games	400m	Finland	1	47.43
8/02/82	Göteborg Invitational	800m	Sweden	3	1:47.33
8/27/82	Van Damme Memorial	800m	Belgium	3	1:46.26
8/31/82	Zürich Weltklasse	800m	Switzerland	?	1:51.40
9/25/82	Oregon Invitational	800m	Eugene	9	1:52.05
10/31/82	Steve Garvey Pepsi Challenge	10k (road)	Santa Monica	?	32:38
1/28/83	Millrose Games	800m	New York	7	1:58.00
2/4/83	Times Indoor Games	4x800	Inglewood	1	(2:00.2 *fell)
2/19/83	Portland Indoor	1000y	Portland	2	2:07.7
2/25/83	TAC Indoors	4x800(p)	New York	1	(1:51.3)
		4x800(f)		1	(1:47.6)
2/27/83	Meadowlands Invitational	1000m	East Rutherford	2	2:21.43
3/26/83	USC All-Comers	400m	Los Angeles	2	47.11
4/02/83	Sun Angel Classic	4x800	Tempe	1	7:12.62(1:46.6)
		SMR(400m)		?	(44.49)
4/24/83	Mt. SAC	800m	Walnut	3	1:47.02
5/15/83	Pepsi Invitational	800m	Westwood	3	1:47.44
5/2183	Volunteer Track Classic	800m(p)	Knoxville	1	1:48.87
		800m(f)		3	1:46.27
5/23/83	Mt. SAC Relays	DMR (800m)	Walnut	1	9:29.3 (1:46.6)
5/24/83		800m		3	1:47.02
		4x400		3	(44.58)
5/28/83	Bruce Jenner Invitational	Mile	San Jose	10	4:13.2
6/12/83	Jumbo Elliott Invitational	800m	Philadelphia	3	1:46.01
6/19/83	TAC Championships	800m	Indianapolis	2	1:44.78
6/26/83	USA vs. GDR dual	800m	Los Angeles	4	1:46.80
7/16/83	Barcelona	800m	Spain	1	1:46.69
7/20/83	Vectis Meeting	800m	Luxembourg	3	1:45.37
8/01/83	Malmö Invitational	800m	Sweden	2	1:46.26
8/07/83	IAAF World Championships	800m(qf)	Finland	1	1:45.84
8/08/83	IAAF World Championships	800m(sf)		4	1:46.39
8/17/83	Berlin ISTAF	800m	Germany	1	1:44.43
8/24/83	Zürich Weltklasse	800m	Switzerland	1	1:44.62

Date	Meet	Event	Location	Place	Time
8/26/83	Van Damme Memorial	800m	Belgium	4	1:45.53
8/28/83	Cologne (1500m WR Maree)	Rabbit	Germany	*	(54.7/1:52.8)
8/31/83	Koblenz	800m	Germany	1	1:44.39
9/01/83	Roma Golden Gala	800m	Italy	1	1:45.70
9/04/83	Rieti (1500m WR Ovett)	Rabbit (1100m)	Italy	*	(54.2/1:51.7)
3/3/84	Long Beach Relays	4x400	Long Beach	1	(44.9)
		200m		1	21.?
4/27/84	Mt. SAC Relays	400m	Walnut	7	48.31
		800m		5	1:49.6
6/06/84	TAC Championships	800m(h)	San Jose	7	1:54.72
6/16/84	Olympic Trials	800m (h)	Los Angeles	4	1:49.21
6/17/84	Olympic Trials	800m(qf)		8	1:56.07
11/12/84	Pico Rivera 15km	15km (road)	Pico Rivera	15	52:29
4/27/85	Mt. SAC Relays	4x800	Walnut	1	7:12.96 (1:47.1)
6/16/85	TAC Championships.	800m	Indianapolis	4	1:44.77
7/16/85	Nice	1000m	France	2	2:17.43
7/19/85	London Talbot Games	800m	England	4	1:45.54
7/23/85	Edinburgh	1000m	Scotland	2	2:16.90
7/27/85	Bislett Games	800m	Norway	DQ	
8/16/85	Bern	800m	Switzerland	1	1:45.79
8/21/85	Zürich Weltklasse	800m	Switzerland	6	1:44.57
8/23/85	Berlin ISTAF	800m	Germany	4	1:44.39
8/25/85	Köln	800m	Germany	7	1:44.49
8/28/85	Koblenz	800m	Germany	3	1:43.35
9/04/85	Rieti	800m	Italy	8	1:49.15
1/17/86	Sunkist Indoor	500y	Los Angeles	5	56.82
1/31/86	Toronto Indoor	1000m	Toronto	2	2:2x.x
2/8/86	Cosford Indoor	1000m	England	?	2:27.76
2/14/86	Millrose Games	800m	New York	5	1:50.58
2/21/86	Times Indoor Games	1000y	Inglewood	3	2:07.3
3/?/86	Cal Poly Invitational	4x400	Pomona	?	(47.56)
4/18/86	Mt. SAC Relays	4x800 (AR)	Walnut	1	7:06.05 (1:46.7)
4/19/86	Bruce Jenner Classic	800m	San Jose	7	1:47.38
5/5/86	Sun Angel Classic	DMR (1200m)	Tempe	1	(2:58.2)
		4x400		2	(47.9)
5/10/86	Modesto Relays	800m	Modesto	3	1:48.36
		4x400		3	(45.01)
5/??/86	Olympic Dev. Meet	1500m	Santa Monica	3	3:49.0
5/17/86	Pepsi Invitational	800m	Westwood	2	1:46.01
5/24/86	SM Dist. Carnival	600m	Santa Monica	3	1:14.15

6/7/86	Prefontaine Invite	800m	Eugene	2	1:45.80
6/21/86	TAC Championships	800m	Eugene	4	1:46.32
8/06/86	Koblenz	800m	Germany	2	1:44.17
8/13/86	Zürich Weltklasse	800m	Switzerland	9	1:46.39
8/15/86	Berlin ISTAF	800m	Germany	?	?
9/02/86	Lausanne Athletissima	800m	Switzerland	9	1:50.69
1/16/87	Sunkist Indoor	1000y	Los Angeles	2	2:08.5
1/30/87	Millrose Games	800m	New York	2	1:51.44
2/14/87	Vitalis Invitational	1000m	East Rutherford	5	2:22.7
5/16/87	Pepsi Invitational	800m	Westwood	?	1:52.04
5/22/87	Santa Monica Twilight	1500m	Santa Monica	4	?:??.??
5/28/87	Seville Invitational	800m	Spain	?	1:49.08
5/30/87	Madrid Invitational	1000m	Spain	?	2:19.19
6/25/87	TAC Championships	800m(p)	San Jose	1	1:48.02
6/26/87	TAC Championships	800m(sf)		2	1:48.38
6/27/87	TAC Championships	800m (f)		3	1:46.49
7/16/87	Paris	800m	France	8	1:46.63
7/18/87	Fanny Blankers Koen Games	800m	Holland	?	1:46.98
7/22/87	Roma Golden Gala	800m	Italy	8	1:47.51
8/13/87	Koblenz	800m	Germany	5	1:45.03
8/21/87	Berlin ISTAF	800m	Germany	?	1:45.70
8/29/87	IAAF World Championships	800m(p)	Italy	4	1:49.47
8/30/87	IAAF World Championships	800m(qf)		7	1:45.68
8/31/87	IAAF World Championships	800m(sf)		6	1:48.49
9/08/87	Rieti	800m	Italy	7	1:59.18
1/22/88	Sunkist Invitational	?	Los Angeles	?	?
1/31/88	Stuttgart Indoor Inv	1000m	Germany	3	?
3/05/88	Manhattan Beach 5k	5k (road)	Manhattan Beach		15:35
3/13/88	Tom Sullivan 10k	10k (road)	Torrance	15	30:58
6/24/88	Lausanne Athletissima	800m	Switzerland	9	1:48.50
7/29/89-	Police and Fire World Games	400m	Vancouver	3	49.34
8/06/89		4x100		1	43.41
		4x400		1	3:22.59

? = unsure of date, performance, place, location...;   y = yards; m = meters; p = prelims;
qf = quarter finals; sf = semi-finals; f= finals; DQ = disqualified; WR = World Record;
AR = American Record; times in ( ) are David's splits

139

Notes

Preface
1. http://www.runningentertainment.com/runningshots7.html
2. John Conrad, "Mack Would Rather Not Be A Duck", *Eugene Register Guard*, March 26, 1980
3. Philip K. Dick, "Beyond Lies the Wub", 1952, https://www.gutenberg.org/files/28554/28554-h/28554-h.htm

Chapter 1
1. https://en.wikipedia.org/wiki/List_of_people_from_Compton,_California
2. comptoncity.org

Chapter 2
1. Thomas Aquinas, *Summa Theologia*
2. Darrell Dawsey, "25 Years After the Watts Riots: McCone Commission's Recommendations Have Gone Unheeded", *Los Angeles Times*. July 8, 1990
3. Erin Blakemore, "How the Black Panthers' Breakfast Program Both Inspired and Threatened the Government" https://www.history.com/news/free-school-breakfast-black-panther-party

Chapter 4
1. Keith R. Conning, http://lynbrooksports.prepcaltrack.com/ATHLETICS/TRACK/STATE_BK/statehis.htm
2. http://www.runningentertainment.com/runningshots7.html
3. http://www.arcadiainvitational.org/
4. https://www.cif-la.org/apps/pages/index.jsp?uREC_ID=49079&type=d&pREC_ID=1245094

Chapter 6
1. http://goducks.com/documents/2018/4/6/Record_Book_4_6_18_.pdf
2. Walter D. Wintle, "It's All In the State of Mind", (public domain), 1905
3. https://news.google.com/newspapers?nid=4pF9x-cDGsoC&dat=19791223&b_mode=2&hl=en

Chapter 7
1. https://news.google.com/newspapers?nid=4pF9x-cDGsoC&dat=19791223&b_mode=2&hl=en

Chapter 8
1. "Dellinger Experiences Stroke During Vacation", *Daily Emerald,* August 7, 2000.
2. *Track and Field News*, December 1982
3. https://news.google.com/newspapers?nid=4pF9x-cDGsoC&dat=19791223&b_mode=2&hl=en
4. "Status Quo", *Track and Field News*, November, 1982

Chapter 9
1. http://digilander.libero.it/atletica2/Stagionali/WRL/1983/800.htm
2. https://en.wikipedia.org/wiki/1983_World_Championships_in_Athletics_%E2%80%93_Men%27s_800_metres
3. Jon Hendershott, *Track and Field News* Nov. 1983
4. *Track and Field News* October. 1983
5. *Track and Field News* October 1983
6. Jon Hendershott, *Track and Field News* Nov. 1983

Chapter 10
1. Bernice Kanner, "Whispering Campaign: Nike's Dramatic Shift", *New York Magazine*, June 25, 1984

Chapter 11
1. https://orthoinfo.aaos.org/en/diseases--conditions/compartment-syndrome/
2. http://www.usatf.org/statistics/champions/olympictrials/historyoftheolympictrials.pdf

Chapter 12
1. http://digilander.libero.it/atletica3/Stagionali/WRL/1985/800.htm
2. Philip Hersch, "Since 1984, There Has Been One Constant In The Finals Of The 800 Meters...", *Chicago Tribune*, July 31, 1996

Chapter 13
1. http://www.mtsacrelays.com/archives/TFN/1986.htm
2. http://digilander.libero.it/atletica2/Stagionali/WRL/1986/800.htm
3. http://www.alltime-athletics.com/index.html

Chapter 14
1. https://en.wikipedia.org/wiki/1987_USA_Outdoor_Track_and_Field_Championships
2. https://en.wikipedia.org/wiki/1987_World_Championships_in_Athletics_%E2%80%93_Men%27s_800_metres
3. http://digilander.libero.it/atletica2/Stagionali/WRL/1987/800.htm
4. http://www.alltime-athletics.com/m_800ok.htm

Chapter 15
1. George Schroeder, "Road From Eugene...", *The Eugene Register Guard*, June 4, 2008
2. https://www.hrw.org/legacy/reports98/police/uspo73.htm
3. https://www.ted.com/talks/chimamanda_adichie_the_danger_of_a_single_story

Chapter 16
1. Martin Luther King Jr., *Strength of Love,* New York : Harper & Row, 1963.

2. https://www.bop.gov/locations/list.jsp
3. **Scott Glover and Matt Lait,** "Ex-LAPD Officer Is Stabbed in Prison", *LA Times*, February 7, 2001
4. **Chuck Philips,** "Informant in Rap Star's Slaying Admits Hearsay", *LA Times,*
   June 3, 2005

Chapter 17
1. http://www.comptonyouthbuild.org/cybmission
2. **Laura Wides,** "Ex-Athlete, 1 Other Dies in Car Crash", *LA Times*, Dec. 21, 2000
3. **"Driver Accused of DUI Arrested in Crash Death of Motorcyclist,"** *LA Times*, Nov. 21, 2011,
4. **Samuel Johnson, quoted in** *The Mother's Assistant,* Vol. VII, No. 2, October 1845
5. https://www.ted.com/talks/chimamanda_adichie_the_danger_of_a_single_story

Epilogue
1. https://en.wikipedia.org/wiki/500_metres

Appendix
1. https://news.google.com/newspapers?nid=4pF9x-cDGsoC&dat=19791223&b_mode=2&hl=en
2. http://www.usatf.org/statistics/champions/olympictrials/historyoftheolympictrials.pdf
3. **Jon Hendershott,** *Track and Field News,* Nov. 1983.
4. http://digilander.libero.it/atletica3/Stagionali/WRL/1985/800.htm
5. http://digilander.libero.it/atletica2/Stagionali/WRL/1986/800.htm
6. http://digilander.libero.it/atletica2/Stagionali/WRL/1987/800.htm
7. https://www.iaaf.org/athletes/united-states/david-mack-7538
8. http://www.cpaf.org/5/index.htm?winscn=Main%7CWPFGResults&win=Main

Photo Credits

Made in the USA
Coppell, TX
28 January 2021

48984408R00089